ROSES

ROSES

S. Millar Gault, MBE, VMH

Sundial

Contents

First published in 1979 by Sundial Publications Limited
59 Grosvenor Street London W1
Second impression, 1979
© 1979 Hennerwood Publications Limited
ISBN 0 904230 75 9
Printed in England by Severn Valley Press Limited

Introduction

ROSES, by tradition England's national flowers, have many qualities which will give pleasure to those who grow them. I know of no other group of plants so diverse in character, which are so easily grown and can be used in so many different ways. Myths are bound to arise around plants so long cultivated in gardens as the rose, but nowadays the myth, or fallacy if you prefer it, that roses will grow only on heavy clay soils has been largely disproved. Fortunately for their many admirers, we know now that roses can be grown on most soils, especially if they are well drained and given good cultivation.

Few prospective rose growers are fortunate enough to have any choice in siting their garden. In general, other considerations have to be given priority, such as convenience of area and type of house. Even the Royal National Rose Society, when it moved to St Albans in Hertfordshire, had to give preference to staff availability and local amenities. The garden soil there is basically a gravel bed, or partly so, and is apt to drain too quickly in summer. However, in spite of this, attention to good cultivation, with some enrichment of the soil before planting, has done much to ensure good results.

Many experienced growers, as well as less experienced and prospective ones, can get much pleasure and information from visits to private and public gardens where roses are a feature. This can be augmented by visiting commercial establishments where roses are a speciality, particularly if these are in easy reach and on similar soil. Varieties you favour can be assessed for performance in those nurseries where a display garden of established roses can be seen. Such visits are invaluable, and will be of even more benefit if they are made when preparatory work is being done.

Commercial growers who have to earn their living from their roses are likely to select land particularly suitable for the production of a valuable crop. Even so, of the many growers I know, all of them cultivate deeply, incorporating farmyard manure, which is supplemented when necessary by suitable proprietary fertilizers. I follow similar methods myself, but use a spade rather than a cultivator.

Rose Types

As a cursory glance at these pages will show, there is an enormous range of roses of different kinds that are suitable for growing in the average garden. It may be helpful at this point, then, to say a few words about classification and about rose types. Roses belong to the genus *Rosa*, which is a member of the great family Rosaceae that includes many other plants, notably many of our favourite fruits.

All the roses we grow in our gardens derive ultimately from wild-growing species. Some of these are native to Britain, but many more have been introduced to this country from distant parts of the world; those native to the Far East, for instance, have been especially important in the development of modern types. The term 'species roses' is applied both to these roses and to their near hybrids – roses that have developed as the result of a cross between two wild-growing species.

One of the most important of the older types of rose is the group known as 'old roses', or 'old garden roses'. These are the result of the work of rose breeders, who developed them from sports (chance variants, or mutants) or from hybrids of species roses. The group includes traditional favourites such as albas, Bourbons, China roses, tea roses, gallicas, damasks, hybrid perpetuals, hybrid sweetbriars, Scotch roses, dwarf polyanthas, rugosas, moss roses, and cabbage roses.

Today the two most popular types of garden roses are the hybrid teas and the floribundas. The hybrid teas originated in France towards the end of the 19th century as a result of crossing two of the most popular old garden roses, hybrid perpetuals and tea roses. Floribundas arose from crossing hybrid teas and dwarf polyanthas. Two other popular types are miniature roses and the modern shrub roses.

Finally, descriptions of roses in this book and others often refer to single, semi-double, and double flowers. These terms refer to the number and arrangement of the petals in each flower. A 'single' rose flower has less than eight petals; most species roses are singles. A 'semi-double' flower has from eight to 20 petals. A 'double' has more than 20 petals.

I hope this book may prove an incentive to those who have not grown roses before, and will provide the more experienced with some new ideas.

A climbing form of the hybrid tea 'Blessings' makes a charming frame to this cottage door.

1 Roses Past and Present

Roses have been grown and much favoured by man for many hundreds of years. An enormous number of books have been written not only about their cultivation but also about their history. This extensive literature can be confusing to the lay reader, particularly so far as the early history of the rose is concerned, and it is evident from these differing accounts that much of that history is based on conjecture.

We are told by geologists that fossils found in rocks provide evidence that the rose goes back in time some 35 million years. By comparison the existence of man can only be traced back about a million years.

Rose species, the wild roses, occur naturally only in the northern hemisphere, where they have a very wide distribution. They range through North America and Europe into North Africa, but the largest number are found in northern Asia, from Siberia to the Himalayas and in China and Japan. Roses are much favoured in Australia and New Zealand and grow well there, but are not found growing wild in either country or in South America. Many of the wild species differ widely; some are dwarfs, while others are mighty climbers up to 12 m (40 ft) in height. Differences in flower, fruit, and foliage also occur, so that botanists are not always in agreement about how many are true species. At the present time a conservative estimate is about 120 species, but only a small proportion of these have played any major part as parents of our modern roses.

The modern hybrid tea is still probably the most popular rose grown in the British Isles for general garden decoration, for it produces the best individual blooms. The wide range of colour, and the beautiful scent of many varieties, make the hybrid tea justly appreciated also by flower arrangers.

Generally 'La France' has been given credit as the prototype of the hybrid tea class, but this is questioned by some authorities who consider 'Brown's Superb Blush' (produced in 1815) has some 50 years' precedence. 'La France', introduced in 1867, was raised by Guillot in France. With its large, fragrant, silvery-pink flowers and recurrent flowering habit it was without doubt the first to display the possibilities of the hybrid tea class. Even today it can be seen occasionally in gardens, although it is now less vigorous than many of our present-day varieties. Unfortunately its fertility was low, but some seedlings were raised, leading on to roses I myself have grown, such as 'Mme Caroline Testout' (still seen in gardens, particularly in its climbing form), and 'Mme Abel Chantenay', a great favourite because of its fragrant pale-pink flowers.

The year 1901 saw the debut of 'Frau Karl Druschki', regarded by some as the first pure-white hybrid tea, but still classified as a hybrid perpetual in *Modern Roses 7* (a check-list of rose names, formed in collaboration with the International Registration Authority for Roses, and put together by The McFarland Company with the American Rose Society). Although it has no scent, 'Frau Karl' became popular and is still seen in older gardens.

Developments in colour

Until this time hybrid tea roses had been pink, red, or white, but a dramatic improvement in the colour range was brought about when Pernet-Ducher, a French nurseryman, succeeded in crossing the semi-double form of the Persian yellow rose *R. foetida persiana* with a red hybrid perpetual, 'Antoine Ducher', which produced the first orange-yellow rose in 1900. This was 'Soleil d'Or', which has red shadings and was at the time classified as a type known as 'pernetiana', after Pernet-Ducher, but is now absorbed in the hybrid teas. When it was crossed with a hybrid tea, 'Mme Melanie Soupert', the first pure yellow cultivar, 'Rayon d'Or', was produced; it was introduced by Pernet-Ducher in 1910.

This breakthrough led to a whole range of new shades when 'Rayon d'Or' was crossed with hybrid teas: oranges, flames, and bicolours with scarlet petals which had a golden-yellow reverse. Unfortunately, they showed a tendency towards weak growth and susceptibility to black spot – characteristics that rose breeders have since tried to eliminate. Less dramatic but of considerable importance, especially for those interested in forcing roses for cut flowers, was the introduction of 'Ophelia' in 1912 by Paul of Waltham Cross. Its beautifully shaped salmon-pink, fragrant flowers and long, pointed buds

'Peace', a hybrid tea rose, has become world famous since its introduction in 1945.

were very much appreciated by rose lovers, not only for home decoration but also in the garden. 'Ophelia' has, in addition, provided so many mutations or sports (in particular 'Madame Butterfly', which also produced 'Lady Sylvia') that, in spite of her unknown parentage, she became the founder of a very large and beautiful family.

The next important breakthrough came when François Meilland, a young French hybridist, produced a seedling which he named 'Mme Antoine Meilland' after his mother. Sufficient stock was ready for distribution in 1939, when World War II intervened. Held back until the war ended, it was launched in America in 1945 with tremendous publicity under the name of 'Peace'. Generally acclaimed for its large blooms of unusual colour (soft yellow, edged with pink), it was considered even more remarkable for its vigour and size. Such a dramatic development led to wide breeding with considerable effect and the production of many good varieties.

In comparatively recent times, in 1943, Wilhelm Kordes, a German breeder, introduced 'Kordes Sondermeldung', which became known in this country and America as 'Independence'. This was the well of colour from which so many of the orange-scarlet floribundas as well as hybrid teas have sprung. 'Independence' had many faults as a garden rose: the blooms flopped on weak stems and as they aged assumed unattractive shades of brick red, so its popularity was brief. Although classified as a floribunda, 'Independence' was really more akin to the hybrid tea type.

'Super Star', raised by another German breeder, Math Tantau, and introduced in 1960, created the next sensation because of its colour, a brilliant light vermilion, which had not been seen in the rose world before. The same raiser introduced 'Duftewolke', better known as 'Fragrant Cloud', four years later and this gained popularity very rapidly owing mainly to its glorious scent, which has defied those who claim that modern roses are without fragrance. In 1972 the English breeder Jack Harkness introduced 'Alexander', a seedling from 'Super Star' even more sensational in its brilliant vermilion red colouring. A Scottish breeder, Alex Cocker, has just

produced 'Silver Jubilee', a most attractive rose with a diffusion of *R. kordesii* in its veins, vigorous and healthy in growth. The flowers are coppery salmon-pink in colour, a subtle blend with further possibilities envisaged.

Hybrid polyanthas

The first dwarf, a polyantha rose, was introduced in 1875 by Guillot of France under the name of 'Paquerette', which had double, white flowers. Produced from *R. multiflora*, the pollen parent is believed to have been a China rose, *R.*

chinensis; both these species had been introduced from the Far East in about 1800. Guillot continued to raise seedlings, and 'Mignonette' was introduced in 1880. From this variety Pernet-Ducher obtained a seedling, 'Mlle Bertha Ludi', which he sent out in 1891 and which is thought to be the first modern hybrid polyantha. The attractive 'Gruss an Aachen' appeared in 1908 and is still grown by some enthusiasts. A year later Levavasseur of Orleans sent out 'Orleans Rose', which

became well known owing to the number of sports which arose from it directly and from its descendants.

Using 'Orleans Rose' as a parent, the Danish nurseryman Svend Poulsen, introduced in 1924 two new hybrid polyanthas, 'Else Poulsen' and 'Kirsten Poulsen'. These attracted a great deal of attention and can still be seen in gardens. They are considered by some authorities to represent the beginning of the hybrid polyanthas which eventually became recognized as floribundas. The advent of 'Karen Poulsen' in 1932 did nothing to lessen the impact of this new race, which proved supremely useful for bedding and for display in

public gardens. A considerable amount of prejudice had to be overcome, for the new type seemed to offer a threat to the supremacy of the hybrid tea.

In 1952 the name 'floribunda' for this class of roses was accepted by the RNRS, although it had been generally used for some years. Edward Le Grice,

Above 'Allgold', a floribunda raised in England in 1956, is one of the finest bedding roses of this colour. **Right** 'Alexander', a hybrid tea introduced in 1972.

a well-known Norfolk breeder, introduced 'Allgold' in 1956, an advance in yellow floribundas, and very healthy and stable in colour. Many raisers all over the world have continued to produce floribunda roses with considerable success. Le Grice in 1969 broke new ground with the first floribunda in purple shades – a combination of the old garden roses allied to the floriferous modern floribunda in the variety 'News'.

The most recent advance has been made by the well-known breeder Sam McGredy IV with his 'hand-painted' series of roses: 'Picasso' in 1971 and 'Matangi' in 1974; while many others are still to be seen.

Miniatures

Miniature roses have a charm all their own, and in recent years there has been a steady increase of interest in this class. Originating from the dwarf form of the China rose, *R. chinensis minima*, the early varieties were the subject of some confusion. 'Pompon de Paris' was grown as a pot plant for the Paris markets around 1840; a variety much like it was brought from Switzerland by a Major Roulet, and is still known as *R. roulettii*. The climbing sport of 'Pompon de Paris' is still grown and is one of the features of the office wall of the Royal National Rose Society's headquarters at St Albans.

In the early 1930s Jan de Vink in Holland and Pedro Dot in Spain made crosses with a range of other roses, mainly hybrid teas and polyanthas, and produced new varieties which retained the miniature habit to a remarkable degree. More recently, in the United States, Ralph Moore has used a wide variety of parents in his breeding programme, and has now succeeded in producing a miniature moss variety called 'Dresden China' and a striped rose called 'Stars 'n' Stripes'.

Above left 'Climbing Pompon de Paris', a sport of a miniature rose of the mid-19th century, makes a fine display in June. It is sometimes catalogued as 'Climbing Rouletii'. **Left** *Rosa kordesii*, a hybrid raised in Wilhelm Kordes' nursery, is the parent of a celebrated race of recurrent-flowering climbers and shrub roses.

Other developments

The rose 'Lady Duncan', introduced in 1900 in America, resulted from a cross between *R. rugosa* and *R. wichuraiana*, both natives of Japan. A trailer which did not attain popularity, 'Lady Duncan' soon disappeared from the catalogues; but it appears to have been resurrected in 1919 and named 'Max Graf'. On its re-introduction into commerce, Wilhelm Kordes planted it, as he was particularly interested in breeding hardy roses. At first he had no success. Eventually, however, in 1940 he obtained seed pods, and from these he raised two seedlings, one of which failed to survive its first winter. The other, however, proved very fertile and has since been recognized as a new species, *R. kordesii*. Crossed with various roses, the result has been a series of repeat-flowering climbers, generally known as the Kordesii climbers, notable for their hardiness and general good health.

The sweet briar, *R. eglanteria*, a native of Britain, has always been much valued for its scented foliage, so it is not surprising that in the late 19th century it became the subject of a serious breeding programme. This was initiated by Lord Penzance and resulted in the introduction, between 1893 and 1895, of several hybrids known collectively as the Penzance briars. They make good shrubs where an impenetrable hedge is required, and possess the characteristic scented leaves.

The hybrid musks (or Pemberton roses, as I prefer to call the group of shrub roses raised by the Rev. G.H. Pemberton between 1912 and 1928) are still among the finest shrub roses for gardens. With their long season of flowering and sweet scent, the Pemberton roses are deservedly favoured by many discriminating gardeners. 'Daphne' was the first to be introduced, and many others followed. 'Belinda' and 'Buff Beauty' were introduced by J.A. Bentall, who succeeded Pemberton, but were most probably raised by the country clergyman himself.

'Parkdirektor Riggers', raised in 1957, is one of the Kordesii climbers, a free-flowering, vigorous grower with strikingly coloured blooms up to 75 mm (3 in) in diameter.

2 The Soil

Soils vary considerably in composition from one part of the country to another; indeed, different types may exist within the compass of a single garden. If you are an inexperienced gardener, or are about to take over a new garden, you would be well advised to have the soil analysed. This can be done by sending samples to a horticultural establishment or, possibly, to your local authority. Alternatively, you can buy a reasonably priced soil-testing kit to determine whether your soil is acid or alkaline.

Roses are reputed to prefer soil that is slightly acid, with a pH of about 6.5. I am inclined to believe that roses in general are fairly tolerant in this respect and that it is more important for the soil to be of a good structure and well supplied with organic matter.

Soil types

For our purposes, soils can be roughly classified as follows.

Clay

Clay soils are both heavy to dig and difficult to cultivate. They are made up of particles so small that water cannot readily pass through them, so that they readily become waterlogged in wet winters. As a result, clay soils are cold and sticky in the spring and are slow to warm up. Little air can get between the particles, and this means that oxygen will be lacking to help in the process whereby organic matter is broken down to form humus. Summer brings further problems: as clay soils dry out, they shrink; this leads to the development of cracks, which encourage further drying and damage to roots, especially in periods of drought.

The structure of clay soils can be improved by inducing the small particles to form into larger crumbs, a process called flocculation. Some gardeners are

tempted to hasten this process by the application of hydrated lime not only to the top spit but to the subsoil as well. Such temptation should be firmly resisted unless analysis has shown the soil to be very acid; lime increases the alkalinity of the soil. Much more suitable is gypsum, which may be forked into the soil at up to 1.5 kg/m² (3 lb/sq yd). The digging in of organic matter, such as partly decayed leaves and strawy manure, in autumn and winter will also considerably improve the texture. These materials, however desirable, are not always readily available, or are in too short supply to fork into the lower spit.

In this case any material such as old newspapers or worn out clothing (if of natural materials) is suitable and will help to open up heavy clay and improve drainage.

Clay soils retain plant foods better than those of lighter texture and are not so subject to leaching (the draining away of nutrients through the soil) in wet winters. Particularly intractable soils can be improved by dressings of rough sedge peat, which should be broken up and well soaked, and of sharp sand.

Chalk

Chalk soils, particularly characteristic of downland, are generally not favoured by prospective rose growers. Such soils are often shallow and drain too freely. In addition they are very deficient in organic matter, so that large quantities of humus-forming material must be worked in when preparing the site. Dedicated rosarians, however, are prepared to accept a challenge, and some have done so with considerable success by excavating much of the chalk with a pick, and replacing it with good topsoil enriched with peat or leaf mould. In general, hybrid tea roses do not thrive on chalk, although quite a few rose species and their hybrids will do so. Pemberton roses and many old garden types, such as hybrid perpetuals, albas, centifolias, and damasks, have proved capable of satisfactory growth in chalk

Above left Inexpensive soil-testing kits are a worthwhile investment for rose-growers.
Right Like most roses, the hybrid tea 'Silver Jubilee' thrives best in slightly acid soil.

soils. Many climbers and ramblers have also been grown successfully, although rugosas, usually so trouble free even in comparatively poor soils, are apt to suffer from iron deficiency in chalk. This shows up as a yellowing of the leaves, known as chlorosis, which can be overcome by dosing with proprietary sequestered iron compounds.

Sand

In terms of digging and cultivation, sandy soils are the opposite of clay, and are also quite different in composition. Their particles, being coarse, do not stick together, and so water drains through them more rapidly – indeed, wastefully so in summer. To counteract this and to help prevent wastage of soluble plant foods, sandy soils should be treated, if at all possible, with heavier types of farmyard manure, from cows or pigs, preferably well rotted. Such material is usually scarce outside country areas and you may have to make do with compost made from garden and kitchen waste. An alternative product is dried compost from sewage sludge and dustbin refuse; this is obtainable from some local authorities, and it is most useful if used in quantity. These latter composts have many advantages as they are free of pests and diseases and contain some essential plant foods. They are generally low in potash, but if pepped up with sulphate of potash they are excellent for roses. In some industrial areas composts from sludge may contain chemicals dangerous to plant life, so you should make sure that any that you wish to acquire is not polluted in this way. In some areas, spent mushroom manure is advertised for sale. This is also beneficial except where, as is quite common, its lime content is very high. In such cases I would not advocate its use on roses.

Excellent roses are grown by many people on light sandy soils, more successfully where plenty of manure or compost has been forked into the subsoil. In very wet winters excessive drainage can be aggravated by autumn cultivation, so if possible it is a good idea to delay cultivation until the spring.

Peat

Although they are high in organic matter, many peat soils are confined to low-lying areas which are so badly drained that they are unsuitable for growing roses. Good drainage is essential; roses object to their roots being kept permanently saturated. High moorland also frequently consists of peat, and again because of bad drainage, as well as of exposure, it too is of little value. Some peat soil is also very acid. I have already mentioned that roses, in my view, are reasonably tolerant so that they can be grown even on fairly acid soils. The addition of lime, especially in the form of ground chalk, will counteract excessive acidity if used at the rate of about 60 g/m² (2 oz/sq yd).

Loam

There can be little doubt that the type of soil generally called loam, in which the clay and sand particles are well balanced, is what most rose growers consider to be ideal. Blessed with such a soil and a high proportion of organic matter, fertility is assured. Most loams have enough body to resist leaching, and beneficial bacteria are more active.

Silt

This type of soil is composed of very fine particles which are inclined to run together and become sticky when wet. After rain, compaction takes place on the surface, forming a hard cement-like crust. This makes cultivation such as hoeing difficult, and any cultivation required is best carried out before the surface has completely dried out. Working in a surface dressing of peat or some humus-forming material, especially if allied to mulching (see page 18), will counteract surface compaction and will generally benefit the plants.

Preparing the soil

I have already indicated that most amateur gardeners have to accept their garden as it stands in relation to the house; but within these limitations it is certainly worth considering the particular requirements of roses. A look at the gardens of neighbouring rose growers is usually very helpful. Most gardeners are willing to talk about their successes – some even about their failures. The latter information, especially if it can be related to local conditions, can be very valuable if you are in your early days as a rose grower.

Roses generally succeed best in open, sunny positions, as long as they have some protection from cold winds from the north or east. If large trees or hedges are used as protection, make sure they are at a sufficient distance to ensure that they do not impoverish the soil, dry it out, or overshade it. Indeed, soil that has been well prepared for roses will itself encourage tree or hedge roots to spread unless a barrier such as corrugated iron or asbestos sheeting is used. You should therefore think carefully before planting trees or vigorous shrubs near your roses. In particular, trees such as weeping willows and poplars should be kept as far as possible from rose beds.

Climatic conditions must also be considered; areas of high rainfall will limit the choice of varieties, and adequate drainage must be ensured. In such areas the large, full-petalled roses usually favoured by exhibitors will be disappointing and so should be avoided. Most roses intended for display are grown in beds or borders cut out of a lawn. The site must be well prepared manually or mechanically and good drainage must be ensured, or results will be disappointing. Generally this can be achieved by thoroughly breaking up the subsoil over the whole area, thus avoiding the creation of a sump where a bed has been made on heavy soil and no drainage outlet is available. If your garden is on heavy land and a local ditch or a drain is available nearby, laying field drainpipes to it will help, especially if you cover the pipes with gravel or other porous material.

In the absence of an outfall, a soakaway at the lowest part of the garden is a suitable alternative. Dig a large hole 1 m (3 ft) in diameter and about twice as deep, replacing the subsoil with broken bricks or hardcore. Cover with turves or brushwood to within about 450 mm (18 in) of the surface, and then fill up with soil. Such a soakaway should be capable of dealing with surface water. These days, and most notably in south-eastern England, so much new building has taken place that drainage, especially in the summer months, has become more than adequate for plant life. Given proper drainage, what really matters is the top spit –

Roses flourish best in sunny positions that are protected against cold winds. This 'Chinatown', a modern shrub rose, has been trained up a south-facing wall.

300 mm (1 ft) – of soil, in which most of the fibrous feeding roots of roses will remain when conditions are to their liking.

It has been customary to advocate deep cultivation for roses. Within reason, this is sound advice, especially if you remember the cardinal principle of keeping the fertile top spit on top and the subsoil below. By all means improve the subsoil by turning it over, breaking it up, and incorporating any organic material you can spare. This is, of course, hard work unless you are young and fit. Personally, having reached an age when I no longer indulge in unnecessary hard work, I confine my efforts to a depth of 600 mm (2 ft) – and then only because my roses are usually planted to remain in the same position for at least 12 years and possibly longer, depending on the variety.

Preparation of the bed by double digging is a simple operation, especially if it is square or rectangular in shape and large enough to enable it to be split into two halves. Remove one spit of soil 450 mm (18 in) wide and 250 mm (10 in) deep from one half and place it at the same end behind the other half. Loose soil can also be cleared. Now dig up the subsoil, using a fork if it is heavy clay. In the case of clay take the opportunity to fork in gypsum at the rate already mentioned. This not only renders the clay more porous, thus improving drainage, but helps to liberate nutrients which will benefit the roses. Gypsum should not be used, however, in well-drained soils.

The next strip of soil can now be turned over on top of the first forked-up strip of subsoil, incorporating with it any organic humus-forming material such as peat, leaf-mould, or farmyard manure. If grass turves have been lifted from a new garden or bed, these should be chopped up and placed on the forked-up lower spit. An organic fertilizer, such as bone meal or hoof-and-horn meal, should also be forked in generously, if you can afford the considerable expense. Peat can be applied to a thickness of 100 mm (4 in). Use the loose soil in the second trench for levelling up the surface of the first strip, and proceed with the work. The last open trench will be filled by the soil removed at the beginning. Do not be alarmed that the level of the bed is higher than

before; it will soon settle, especially if a few rainstorms occur. This preparatory work is best done in early autumn, to allow some consolidation of the soil before planting takes place. I hope you will not regard all this work as being too laborious. Remember it is only before planting that such an opportunity occurs and, as you enjoy your roses over many years, you will come to regard it as time and effort well spent.

Deep cultivation by digging on light sandy soil is not really advisable, especially if the subsoil is also sandy, because digging will further increase the drainage and so will reduce the moisture content to unacceptable levels in summer. Rather than disturb the subsoil, concentrate your efforts on making the top spit more water-retentive by adding manure, chopped turf, heavy topsoil, or any other humus-forming material. A heavy dressing of bonemeal and/or hoof-and-horn meal will help to repair the shortage of nutrients. A generous mulch of peat or compost after planting will help to conserve moisture. On light soils it is also advantageous to keep the finished surface of the bed somewhat lower than the surrounding area, especially if irrigation in summer is required, as this ensures the roses receive the full benefit.

While this preparatory work is going on it is a good idea to have a few sacks or a polythene sheet to protect the surrounding grass and minimize clearing up. The same sheet can be used later to protect the bed from frost or heavy rain before planting.

Mulching preserves soil moisture and helps to protect roots against extreme cold.

Mulching

The roots through which roses derive their nourishment are, in the main, the fibrous ones which grow near the surface of the soil. It takes only a few weeks of very dry weather in spring, especially in light soils, to make you appreciate why soil moisture must be conserved. Mulching – spreading a layer of material over the bed between the plants – will conserve not only moisture but also food and, in addition, it will protect the precious roots from extreme coldness of the soil caused by harsh, drying winds during the early weeks of spring.

The mulch should preferably be loose in texture so it will not prevent air getting to the roots. If you use well-made garden compost or farmyard manure as a mulch it should be well broken down before applying to a thickness of 50 mm (2 in) all over; this will also provide additional food. It is best to apply the mulch before too much development has taken place in the young growth of the roses: mid-April can be taken as a general guide. Too early an application will keep the soil too cold.

Many materials can be used for mulching, but if they are short of plant nutrients it is a good idea to give first a dressing of one of the compound fertilizers specially prepared for roses.

Peat has become very popular as a mulch, but it must be well soaked before applying; if it is applied dry, rain has difficulty in penetrating it, and it is also apt to blow away in strong winds.

Lawn mowings are frequently used, for mulching is a convenient means of disposal, saving many journeys to the compost heap; but do not use them if you have treated your lawn with a selective weed-killer. Unfortunately, many lawns include annual meadow grass (*Poa annua*) in their composition, and this will readily take root. In general, then, there is much to be said for consigning mowings to the compost heap and allowing them to become thoroughly composted before applying them to the rosebed. But if you do use them straight from the lawn, sprinkle them thinly over the bed so as not to form an impenetrable mat over the surface. Spent hops are also useful for mulching or improving the soil. Pulverized bark has received much publicity in recent times because of its value in horticulture, and it has been widely used as a mulch. In its favour is its appearance; it is better looking than lawn mowings, and it is less attractive to birds than farmyard manure. Opinions differ about its effect on the soil, but it is worth a trial if you can afford it.

Compost

Owing to the shortage of farmyard manure, particularly in towns, compost has become almost a cult with some gardeners, and many strange mixtures and concoctions are favoured. However, if all house and garden waste of animal or vegetable origin is saved and decomposed, much useful material will be made available both for improving the soil and for mulching. Much has been written about compost by fanatics as well as by many level-headed horticulturists. As a good supply of organic material is of great importance in the growing of roses, a few remarks about the principles involved in its production deserve a place here.

It is a considerable advantage to have at least two compost bins. Their bases should be open on the soil, and their sides should have openings to allow air to penetrate and encourage useful bacteria in their work of decomposing the

waste materials. The material is best introduced in layers about 120 mm (5 in) deep; if possible close-packing materials such as lawn mowings should alternate with looser materials such as straw, bracken, garden waste, and so on. Sprinkle on some lime every few layers. It will also help to add a little manure or some soil containing a nitrogenous fertilizer. Very dry materials such as straw or old hay should be dampened, but do not soak the mass as this will impede the circulation of air; the top of the compost bin should have a cover to keep out heavy rain.

The compost should be built up layer by layer to a height of about 1 m (3 ft). When the compost in the first container shows signs of becoming decomposed, it should be transferred to another. When doing this make sure

Most of the food needs of roses can be provided by compost, and city rose-growers especially can save money and time by making their own from vegetable waste.

that the less-well composted material from the top and sides is put in the middle and is covered by the most highly decomposed. Fresh material, as it becomes available, should be placed in the first container. When the compost is used for roses, either as a soil improver or for mulching, it is advisable to add a few handfuls of sulphate of potash in order to balance up the nutrient value. The finished product should be a dark brown powder, easy to apply and spread – not the glutinous, smelly mess that sometimes passes for compost.

Double digging. Remove the first spit.

Break up heavy subsoil with a fork.

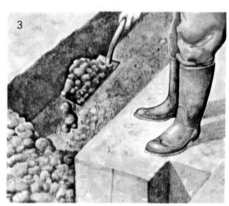

Fill first spit with topsoil from second.

Fill second spit with topsoil from first.

3 Planting and Feeding

IN larger rose nurseries today much of the lifting and trimming of top growth is done mechanically. Some growers no longer wait for an early frost to cause shedding of leaves but deal with this by other means, so that the purchaser does not have the tedious job of removing leaves when the plants arrive from the nursery. Packing methods have also been improved. No longer do the plants arrive in strawed bundles; now they are in polythene or paper bags stitch-closed by machine.

Care of new plants

On arrival the plant packages should be opened carefully, the plants examined for damage to growth or roots, and any damaged parts removed by cutting back to sound wood. If the roots are very long it is better to shorten them back to 250 mm (10 in) or thereabouts. If your soil is not ready for planting or conditions are not favourable, it is better to 'heel in' the plants in a spare part of the garden. This entails taking out a trench, putting the plants in separately and covering up the roots and bottom part of the stems with soil, firming it a little to ensure that they do not dry out. If the roots are dry they should be immersed in water beforehand for several hours: roses that are planted in a very dry state are unlikely to prosper.

Many rose nurserymen include hints on the package about the treatment required on arrival, and the advice offered is normally sound and should be followed. Roses sometimes arrive at times which are inconvenient to the buyer; for instance, the ground may be too wet, or frozen, or covered with snow. In such cases you may have to cover the roots with compost or protect them with straw in a shed or garage until conditions improve. If you have bought a mixed collection of roses, as beginners often do, and find them identified with card or paper labels, it is better to replace these with plastic or some other durable type of label. If the consignment becomes delayed in transit the roses may arrive looking dry and shrivelled. Burying them in a trench a spit deep and covering them with soil for about a week will generally restore them. They can then be uncovered, lifted, and planted in the normal way. If long delays occur in delivery or the roses are badly damaged or diseased, let the nurseryman know as soon as possible. He has a reputation to uphold and if the fault clearly lies with him he will probably replace the plants. Most nurserymen publish conditions of sale, and you should read these carefully to know where you stand.

Large numbers of roses are now sold in stores in packs which are designed to prevent drying out of the roots. Some of these packs are designed to make it easy for the purchaser to examine the plant and its roots. Such plants should be bought as soon as possible after they are delivered to the store. Avoid those which have lain around for some time in a heated building: the tell-tale signs include pale, colourless stems and new roots.

Bare-root roses

Correct planting of bare-root plants (that is, those not grown in containers) is an important aspect of rose growing, especially since the plant may remain in the same place for several years. Planting can take place from late October to the end of April, depending on the area and soil conditions. I prefer autumn planting, in October and November, when there is still some warmth in the soil. In colder areas, and especially in exposed gardens, it is often better to wait until March, when there will be better weather ahead. Avoid planting when snow covers the ground or when it is waterlogged or frozen. Mulching the bed with peat and covering it with polythene will do much to compensate for bad soil conditions, and will allow planting to proceed when the weather is congenial.

Many growers find it worth while before planting to immerse the top growth in a weak solution of a sterilizing agent such as Jeyes Fluid, especially in areas where rose diseases are known to be troublesome.

The planting operation itself is quite simple. Avoid digging out a small hole in a hurry and squeezing the roots into it. Roses are tough plants and may well survive such treatment, but their development could be delayed.

When plants arrive from the nurseryman check them carefully for damage, where necessary cutting growths back to sound wood.

Assuming your soil is in good condition for planting, it is a sound idea to prepare a mixture of granulated peat which is moist but not sodden. To each large bucketful of peat add a double handful of a slow-acting organic fertilizer. Sterilized bone meal is often recommended, but even better (if you can afford the extra expense) is hoof-and-horn or meat-and-bone meal. Now take out a hole 300 mm (12 in) across and deep enough to ensure that the point of union of the stock and scion will be 25 mm (1 in) below the surface of the soil. Place a double handful of the peat and fertilizer mixture into the hole, place the plant on this, spreading the roots fan-wise, and then add more of the mixture. Shake the roots gently (or, better still, get a helper to do so) as you fill in the hole. If help is not available, use a forked stick to hold the rose in its correct position until the soil is gently firmed in. Firming should be done by treading the soil against the roots.

A neat job is easier to achieve if you place sticks or markers at the appropriate distances before planting. A distance of 300 mm (1 ft) should be allowed from the edge of the bed to the first row of plants to enable a mower to cut the grass without damaging the roses. Planting distances will vary according to the vigour of the variety, its habit, and also the ideas of the grower. My own preference is for intervals of about 450 mm (18 in) either way, but I allow an extra 150 to 300 mm (6 to 12 in) for the stronger growers or where a few ground-cover plants are to be grown between the roses. I do not find that wide planting gives a pleasing effect, for bare soil has little appeal, especially in high summer. The effect is also much better if the plants are staggered, rather than in straight lines, and this is most easily done if at least three rows of plants can be accommodated. In this case, the centre row will be planted mid-way between the outer rows. In a rectangular bed, the outer rows should be arranged to fill the corners, which will give an impression of greater depth.

Standard or half-standard roses may be planted to give height to the beds and to increase their effect. In this case the standards should be placed in position before the other roses, and good stakes inserted so that the plants can be placed against them. Avoid driving in the stake after planting, as you will most likely damage the roots. The roots of standards on rugosa stock sometimes require attention before planting, as deep planting of rugosas encourages the production of suckers. If they have several tiers of roots, remove the uppermost ones cleanly; those at the base should be planted no more than 100 mm (4 in) below the surface. Temporary support should be given by a loose tie to the stake, allowing some weeks for the soil to consolidate before tying permanently. This also applies to climbing and rambler roses. If they are allowed permanently to hang loose, wind can cause rocking, which will damage the new and delicate root fibres that are just emerging into the soil.

Late Planting

In northern and colder gardens, planting may not be possible until April. In such circumstances it is better to prune before planting, doing so quite severely to a couple of eyes and removing all weak stems (*see* Chapter 12). Puddling the roots before planting in a 'porridge' of clayey soil and water, mixed up on the ground or in a container, will help to prevent drying out, especially on light soils. Planting will be easier if you can persuade a friend to hold the plants in position until you have firmed them in the soil. A surface mulch of moist peat or compost should be applied immediately to prevent loss of soil moisture and, if the weather is dry, watering may also be necessary.

Container-grown roses

Nowadays planting of container-grown rose bushes has become very popular. It is especially useful if an existing plant has failed and a gap in the bed needs to be filled. This method also enables planting to be carried out when weather conditions are most favourable to the planter.

The soil should be prepared as for bare-root roses. The plant should of course be healthy in appearance and have made good growth; ensure that the roots are moist and, if they are not, give them a thorough watering and allow them to drain before removing the container. The planting hole should be dug out and the container placed in it to ensure that when planted the root ball will be below the surface of the surrounding soil. Most containers are of polythene and can be cut down with a sharp knife and then peeled off the ball of soil. This ball must be kept intact, so it must be handled carefully. Fill in the gap between the root-ball soil and surrounding soil gently but firmly to ensure they are in contact. In hot weather a good soaking of water is recommended; the surplus should be allowed to drain off before the soil is levelled.

Transplanting

Many amateurs grow a mixture of rose varieties. In such a scheme it may sometimes be necessary to move some bushes because colours clash or because a particular bush is too high, too low, or too spreading in habit. Such transplanting is best carried out in late October or November. You will have to dig a larger hole to accommodate the increased roots of a mature plant. When lifting the bush try to keep as many of the fibrous roots as possible in the ball of soil. Long, anchoring roots are likely to be damaged to some extent, but they can be shortened back before replanting.

If transplanting is done quickly, no great check is suffered, and any damage can be overcome, to some extent, by fairly hard pruning.

Healthy rose beds

Amateur gardeners are often disappointed by the effects of their attempts to refurbish old rose beds by the introduction of some young plants. The usual cause of such disappointment is that the beds have been filled with roses for several years and have become 'rose-sick'. This condition may be overcome by a system used by the RNRS at St Albans, where many roses are grown for trial. The system involves grassing down beds of rose-sick soil and bringing intervening grass paths under cultivation for the next period. In a garden this would involve grassing down the old bed and cutting out a new one, which might not be practicable. Changing the topsoil is another possibility if the garden is large enough but this is a laborious job. Another alternative is to use a proprietary soil sterilant. If you do so, be careful to follow the instructions on the container.

When planting has been finished, the soil should be forked through and levelled up so as to leave the top 25 mm (1 in) loose. If you have planted in autumn, you should make an occasional inspection of the new-planted bushes to ensure that they have remained firm: severe frost or high winds may loosen them, in which case you should firm them in by treading when the soil surface is dry.

Feeding

Where care has been taken to follow the methods of preparation advocated, little if any further feeding should be necessary until the second year after planting. Where adequate moisture is available either from rainfall or irrigation I think it is often beneficial to encourage the roses to produce fibrous roots and establish themselves well before trying to improve their performance. Roses, particularly the hybrid tea and floribunda groups, have the reputation of being gross feeders, and it is true that in general they will respond to generous treatment. Strong growth, large, richly coloured flowers, and handsome foliage will result in due course.

Newly planted roses sometimes suffer a setback, particularly if they are planted late and bad weather, especially cold winds and sudden drought, prevails that spring. In such cases, it is a good idea to feed the roses with a fast-acting fertilizer.

The three most important elements for satisfactory plant growth are nitrogen (N), phosphorus (P), and potash (K). Nitrogen encourages growth, especially of foliage, but if it is over-used or applied too late in the season it can cause soft sappy growth, especially in wet years. Such growth is unlikely to resist disease or to ripen well and it renders some varieties prone to die back. The nitrogenous fertilizers include sulphate of ammonia, nitrate of soda, and granular forms such as nitro-chalk. This last acts quickly, is easily applied, and will not adhere to the foliage (so lessening the risk of scorched leaves); being chalky, it will not increase the acidity of the soil.

Fertilizers containing phosphate encourage development of a fibrous root-system, help growths to mature, and so lead to hardier plants. Winter hardiness is important if roses are grown in exposed gardens or if rainfall is high. The chief phosphate fertilizers are super-phosphate, steamed bone flour, and bone meal; this last, which must be sterilized before it is used is now very expensive.

'Harry Wheatcroft', like most other hybrid teas, is a gross feeder and should be fed generously after it has become established in its first two years.

Potash is vital to roses, especially on light or chalky soils, and helps to counteract soft growth and aids ripening. The main potash fertilizers are sulphate of potash and muriate of potash; the latter is *not* recommended for roses. Most rosarians find general compound mixtures (containing nitrogen, phosphorus, and potash) convenient, particularly those specially prepared for roses. If you use mixtures, make sure their potash content is high.

A variety of 'trace elements' are also necessary to plant growth. These are available in various proprietary preparations. They are also present in good farmyard manure (if you are lucky enough to have a source of supply); moreover, this manure helps additionally by improving the structure of your garden soil.

Organic manures should be applied early in the season before growth starts as their nutrients are released slowly over the season. Dried blood is much quicker acting, but it is now too expensive to be used as a general fertilizer by most amateur gardeners.

When you buy compound fertilizer mixtures make sure that they have a guaranteed analysis, showing the exact proportions in which the materials are available. Bear in mind that the *insoluble* proportion of each material present is virtually useless: the plant is capable of absorbing only those materials that have dissolved in the soil water.

Feeding is best carried out when the soil is damp. If you have to feed your roses in dry weather, water the soil first, then apply the fertilizer and water it in. Always follow the instructions of the fertilizer manufacturer. Overfeeding is not merely wasteful: it may harm your roses.

A simple feeding programme to follow is to apply a rose compound after pruning, pricking this lightly into the soil surface with a fork – an operation which also tidies up the bed. Another dressing may be given when the first crop is over and the dead flowers have been removed. It is important that this second dressing should have a high potash content and I have found a fish meal with extra potash to be very effective. If you can afford it, an autumn application of sterilized bone meal will provide a long-lasting benefit as it is slow in action.

4 Hybrid Tea Roses

MANY of the more traditional rosarians regard the hybrid tea as the aristocrat of the rose world – although floribunda enthusiasts are inclined to dispute this. If you like a rose to be of classic formation, with a high pointed centre and petals which reflex gracefully, then this is the group to which you will turn. Many of our modern hybrid teas flower freely enough to make a good garden display, and if they are disbudded they will produce even larger blooms. In spite of the belief that old roses are more fragrant, most hybrid teas have some scent and many can claim this as a feature.

Making a selection can be difficult. I am familiar mainly with roses growing in British gardens, and naturally my choice is biased in this direction. Even within these confines some varieties are more suited than others to particular districts. For instance, large-flowered doubles with a great number of petals are likely to ball (fail to open) in areas of high rainfall.

Average planting distance for all the following is 60 cm (2 ft) apart either way. The height given for each cultivar is only an approximation since it will depend greatly on the area you live in, soil conditions, and pruning methods.

Selection

'Admiral Rodney', 1 m (3 ft). A large-flowered favourite for exhibition, pale rose-pink with slightly deeper reverse to petals.

'Alec's Red', 1 m (3 ft). Strong and upright in growth. Large, full, very fragrant, cherry-red flowers are produced freely.

'Alexander', 1.5 m (5 ft). A very tall, upright grower; flowers somewhat thin in petalage but a striking vermilion in colour. Good for an informal hedge.

'Alpine Sunset', 800 mm (2½ ft). A good grower of medium height; the

large peach-pink flowers have a yellow flush and are scented.

'Big Chief', 1.1 m (3½ ft). Strong and upright in growth; huge crimson flowers with long-lasting qualities. An exhibitor's variety which requires protection from rain.

'Blessings', 1 m (3 ft). A most attractive bedding rose, with bushy growth; the soft coral-pink flowers are freely produced and are pleasantly fragrant.

'Blue Moon', 1 m (3 ft). Moderate in growth, at present the best of the so-called 'blue roses' for garden use; the well-formed silvery lilac flowers are strongly fragrant.

'Bobby Charlton', 1 m (3 ft). A vigorous upright grower; the large, deep-pink blooms have a silvery reverse. An exhibitor's variety.

'Bonsoir', 1 m (3 ft). A healthy grower producing attractive peach-pink flowers freely. Suitable for exhibition and scented, but sensitive to rain damage.

'Champion', 800 mm (2½ ft). A medium-sized plant which produces very large, perfectly shaped blooms of creamy gold with flushes of pink and crimson. Useful in the garden and ideal for the exhibitor; scented.

'Cheshire Life', 600 mm (1½ ft). Grows well and produces its vermilion-orange flowers freely. Resistant to bad weather.

'Coalite Flame', 1 m (3 ft). Vigorous and upright in growth; the deep, glowing, vermilion flowers are fragrant.

'Dekorat', 1 m (3 ft). A vigorous shrubby grower; the coral blooms, tinged with pale gold, are large and fragrant.

'Diorama', 1 m (3 ft). A good bedding rose; its apricot-yellow fragrant flowers resist bad weather conditions.

'Doris Tysterman', 1 m (3 ft). Tall, vigorous, and upright in growth; the flowers are orange-red. It is somewhat vulnerable to mildew.

Above left 'Alpine Sunset'. **Right** 'Double Delight', especially noted for its scent.

Above The subtly tinted 'Blue Moon', with a striking scent. **Below** The perfect form of 'Grandpa Dickson'.

'Double Delight', 800 mm (2½ ft). A medium-sized plant with most distinctive blooms, attractively formed, creamy white in colour with strawberry-red edges to the petals, and wonderfully fragrant.

'Ena Harkness', 1 m (3 ft). A famous rose, with crimson-scarlet fragrant flowers, freely produced. Requires good cultivation.

'Ernest H. Morse', 1 m (3 ft). A sturdy upright grower which makes a good bedding rose; its dark red, scented flowers are freely produced.

'Evening Star', 1.2 m (4 ft). A tall variety, producing finely shaped, long-lasting white flowers.

'Fragrant Cloud', 1 m (3 ft). A popular variety for bedding; its gloriously scented geranium-red flowers acquire purplish tinges as they age in hot weather. Vigorous in growth, it may require protection against black spot.

'Fred Gibson', 1.1 m (3½ ft). A tall, erect grower; flowers of classical formation, amber-yellow to apricot. An exhibitor's favourite.

'Grandpa Dickson', 1 m (3 ft). A very upright grower; produces large, lemon-yellow flowers of true classical shape. Much favoured by exhibitors, and also good for gardens.

'Harry Wheatcroft', 800 mm (2½ ft). A sport from 'Piccadilly'; flamboyant orange-red flowers with yellow stripes. It has the excellent bedding habit of its parent (see below).

'John Waterer', 1.1 m (3½ ft). A tall, erect grower of good bedding habit; its large rosy-red flowers are freely produced. Slightly scented.

'Josephine Bruce', 600 mm (2 ft). A somewhat sprawling grower that requires pruning to an inward-facing eye (see Chapter 13); glowing, velvety crimson flowers of good form and fragrance. Prone to mildew.

'Just Joey', 800 mm (2½ ft). A fairly vigorous, upright grower; large coppery orange flowers with marked red veins – a very popular colour.

'King's Ransom', 800 mm (2½ ft). A compact grower; freely produces medium-sized, rich yellow flowers. A good bedder.

'Korp', 1 m (3 ft). A very upright grower; its flowers, small, neat, and mainly single, are a striking signal red and vermilion in colour. Long lasting, and good for cut flowers.

'Litakor' ('Lolita'), 1 m (3 ft). A good grower, most popular for cut flowers, and very productive; perfectly formed coppery gold flowers. Useful also as a garden plant.

'Mala Rubinstein', 1.1 m (3½ ft). A strong, tall grower; very freely produced coral-pink flowers with a deeper reverse, and gloriously fragrant.

'Mischief', 1 m (3 ft). A first-class rose for bedding; its medium sized, soft coral-salmon flowers are freely produced and resistant to rain.

'Mme Louis Laperrière', 800 mm (2½ ft). A moderate grower which is excellent for bedding; its dark crimson flowers, richly perfumed, are produced early and over a long season.

'Mullard Jubilee', 1.2 m (4 ft). A very robust grower, superb for large beds; its deep rose-pink flowers, freely produced, are large and fragrant.

'National Trust', 800 mm (2½ ft). A neat, compact grower of ideal bedding habit; its medium-sized, well-formed, deep crimson-scarlet flowers are freely produced.

'Papa Meilland', 800 mm (2½ ft). A plant of medium vigour; its dark, velvety crimson, perfectly shaped flowers have a superb fragrance. Very prone to mildew.

'Pascali', 1.1 m (3½ ft). A tallish grower; produces its creamy white flowers freely. One of the few whites resistant to rain. Useful as a cut flower.

'Peace', 1.2 m (4 ft). A famous rose of robust growth and still popular; its freely produced, enormous flowers are yellow flushed with pink, paling as they age. Little scent.

'Peer Gynt', 1 m (3 ft). A vigorous, compact grower; full, somewhat globular flowers of canary yellow, flushed with pink as they age. Almost continuously in bloom.

'Piccadilly', 800 mm (2½ ft). A compact, bushy grower which has attracted popularity because of its scintillating appearance; freely produced flowers, scarlet with yellow reverse. An excellent bedding variety.

'Pink Favourite', 800 mm (2½ ft). A vigorous, healthy grower with most handsome foliage; large, excellently shaped, rose-pink flowers. A good variety for garden and exhibition, it is somewhat late in flowering and is resistant to disease.

'Pascali' makes a delightful cut flower.

'Pink Supreme', 1.1 m (3½ ft). A vigorous, branching grower with characteristically long stems; it freely produces medium-sized, bright-pink flowers on long stems. May require protection against black spot.

'Precious Platinum', 1 m (3 ft). A vigorous grower; it freely produces scented, well-formed crimson blooms. An excellent bedding variety.

'Prima Ballerina', 1 m (3 ft). A very vigorous, upright grower; its freely produced, richly fragrant, deep cherry-pink flowers pale with age. Tends to get mildew.

'Red Devil', 1.1 m (3½ ft). A tall, vigorous plant; enormous, glowing-scarlet flowers with a lighter reverse, ideal in shape and scented. Very popular for exhibition. Requires protection from rain.

'Rose Gaujard', 1.1 m (3½ ft). A very vigorous, spreading grower; large, full, white flowers, heavily flushed with carmine, with a silvery reverse. An ex-

Left 'Red Devil', noted for its glossy foliage.
Below 'Whisky Mac' is unusually fragrant for a rose of this colour.

cellent variety for the beginner, it is easy to grow into an outstanding plant, but its mixture of colours is not to everyone's taste.

'Silver Jubilee', 800 mm (2½ ft). A most vigorous, healthy grower; large, coppery salmon-pink flowers with peach shading, slightly scented. The flowers are freely produced over a long season, generally singly.

'Sunsilk': *see* Chapter 5.

'Super Star', 1 m (3 ft). This luminous vermilion rose was the first of its colour to be introduced and enjoyed enormous popularity until recently. It is, however, susceptible to mildew in some areas and it is not recommended to the amateur grower.

'Sutter's Gold', 1 m (3 ft). An upright grower, excellent for cut flowers when established; its orange-red buds open into light orange-yellow flowers. An older variety which disperses its scent freely. Requires well-cultivated soil.

'Sweet Promise' ('Sonia'), 1 m (3 ft). A fairly vigorous, branching grower; shapely, moderate-sized, fragrant flowers of a delicate salmon-pink

colour. Suitable for cut-flower production under glass.

'Troika', 1 m (3 ft). A vigorous, healthy, upright grower; its shapely and pleasantly fragrant light-apricot blooms deepen into orange at the edges.

'Typhoon', 800 mm (2½ ft). A vigorous, upright grower and an excellent bedding plant; slightly fragrant salmon-pink flowers with orange shadings.

'Wendy Cussons', 1 m (3 ft). A vigorous, branching grower; full, classically shaped, deeply fragrant cerise-scarlet blooms. A very reliable bedder, it may require protection against black spot.

'Whisky Mac', 800 mm (2½ ft). A very compact grower; medium-sized, fragrant blooms of amber and bronze. Liable to mildew in some areas.

'Yellow Pages', 1.2 m (4 ft). A tall, upright plant; slightly fragrant, bright-yellow blooms flushed with pink. A useful bedding variety, it is easier to grow than many other yellows.

Right 'Yellow Pages' makes a good bedding rose. **Below** 'Typhoon', another good bedder, has a delicate fragrance.

5 Floribunda Roses

D URING the last 20 years there has been a phenomenal increase in the number of floribunda roses introduced into cultivation. The term 'floribunda' has no significance botanically; it is used merely to designate a group of roses that develop flowers in clusters. Breeders have produced a section of this group with larger, semi-double flowers, known as floribunda/hybrid tea type, which is confusing to the amateur gardener and in particular to the newcomer to rose growing. Extensive breeding between the classes has in fact resulted in so many borderline varieties that even experts sometimes find classification bewildering.

Floribunda roses as a class must be free-flowering throughout the season, thus providing continuous colour. It is this quality which has made the type so popular in recent years, and explains why it has been used in increasing numbers in public parks and gardens. Amateurs who appreciate colour in the mass have also turned to this type, for they know they can expect to find secondary growths developing before the first truss of bloom has completely finished.

The list of varieties which follows is in the main confined to those of fairly recent introduction in order to avoid, if possible, adding to the confusion of the beginner. Any list must be subject to some reservations, not least because tastes differ. Indeed, one of the many joys of gardening in general and rose growing in particular is the element of personal choice. With floribundas the range to choose from is wide indeed.

Selection

'Allgold', 800 mm (2½ ft). A compact grower, moderate in vigour; semi-double flowers of a bright buttercup yellow which does not fade. An early flowering variety that withstands rain and is resistant to disease.

'Anne Cocker', 1 m (3 ft). An up-

right, vigorous grower; light vermilion blooms in a rosette formation of distinctive appearance. Rather late to flower, it lasts well as a cut flower; inclined to mildew in some areas.

'Apricot Nectar', 1 m (3 ft). A vigorous, bushy grower; delightful pinkish apricot flowers with yellow base; slight scent.

'Arthur Bell,' 1 m (3 ft). Vigorous and upright in growth; large, bright-yellow flowers when young, later fading to cream. One of the most fragrant floribundas; rain resistant.

'Bonfire Night', 1 m (3 ft). Bushy and upright in growth; bright-orange flowers splashed with yellow. A brilliantly coloured bedder which requires watching for black spot.

'Busy Lizzie', 800 mm (2½ ft). Compact and bushy in growth; prolific pastel-pink flowers. An excellent variety for bedding.

'City of Belfast', 800 mm (2½ ft). Free and bushy in growth; freely produces large trusses of bright vermilion-scarlet. An excellent bedder flowering over a long season, it is weather resistant and slightly fragrant.

'City of Leeds', 1 m (3 ft). Upright and vigorous in growth; neat, freely produced, rich salmon-pink blooms. A fine bedder, it is prone to rust in some areas.

'Dame of Sark', 1 m (3 ft). A healthy, easily grown variety; rich orange, red, and orange-yellow flowers. One of the most striking floribundas suitable for bedding.

'Dearest', 800 mm (2½ ft). Vigorous and bushy in growth; beautiful fragrant, soft salmon-pink flowers. One of the more popular fair-weather floribundas, it is less happy in the rain, and it has a tendency to mildew.

'Elizabeth of Glamis', 800 mm (2½ ft). A moderate grower which does not

Above left 'Arthur Bell', a notably scented floribunda. Right The distinctively coloured single flowers of 'Eye Paint'.

take kindly to cold, heavy soil, or exposed sites; beautiful fragrant, salmon-pink flowers infused with apricot. Should be watched for disease.

'English Miss', 800 mm (2½ ft). Grows with a distinctive branching habit; large sprays of fragrant, pale-pink, camellia-shaped flowers.

'Escapade', 1 m (3 ft). A very vigorous grower; fragrant flowers of light

to black spot in some areas.

'Gardener's Sunday', 1.1 m (3½ ft). A tall, bushy grower; fragrant, well-formed, bright-yellow flowers. A good hedger.

'Glenfiddich', 1 m (3 ft). A good, upright grower; flowers are a lovely golden amber in cooler northern gardens, but paler in hot southern gardens.

'Harking' ('Judy Garland'), 1 m

'Iceberg', 1.2 m (4 ft). Vigorous and upright; medium-sized white flowers, occasionally flushed with pink. Justly celebrated as a standard, it bears flowers in profusion throughout a long growing season.

'Iced Ginger', 1.1 m (3½ ft). Very upright in growth; shapely budded flowers in a blend of apricot, buff, and deep copper. Ideal as a cut flower.

magenta paling off in the centre. A weather-resistant variety especially suitable for an informal hedge or large bed.

'Evelyn Fison', 800 mm (2½ ft). Vigorous and branching in growth; vivid red flowers produced throughout the season. A popular bedding variety with good weather resistance.

'Eye Paint', 1.2 m (4 ft). Vigorous and bushy; delightful single, scarlet flowers with a white eye. Good for large beds or informal hedges; prone

(3 ft). A bushy and vigorous variety; freely produced, slightly fragrant, deep-yellow-edged orange flowers.

'Harkuly' ('Margaret Merril'), 1 m (3 ft). Vigorous and branching in growth; small, well-formed white flowers faintly sheened with pale pink. It has one of the most exquisite fragrances of all the roses.

'Harry Edland', 800 mm (2½ ft). A vigorous, bushy grower; full, fragrant, deep-lilac flowers. Grows better than many other lilac-coloured floribundas.

'Iced Ginger', with its subtly blended shades of colour, is one of the longest-lasting of the floribundas when used as a cut flower.

'Kerryman', 1 m (3 ft). A vigorous grower; large pink blooms, darker at the edges. Will flower freely over a long season.

'Korresia', 1 m (3 ft). Medium-sized bushy grower; shapely, fragrant, bright-yellow flowers which do not fade. One of the best garden varieties among the floribundas.

ates well with 'News' (below); flowers over a long season and is especially attractive in autumn.

'News', 800 mm (2½ ft). A robust, compact grower; free-flowering, open, beetroot-red blooms changing to purple. Its effect is enhanced if combined with pale-yellow roses or with grey-foliaged plants.

'Old Master', 800 mm (2½ ft). Of medium height, vigorous in growth; slightly fragrant, carmine-purple flowers with silvery white reverse.

'Paddy McGredy', 600 mm (2 ft). A compact grower; abundant hybrid-tea-shaped carmine-pink flowers touched with salmon, and slightly scented; abundant glossy dark-green foliage. Effective for bedding. May need protection against black spot.

'Pernille Poulsen', 800 mm (2½ ft). Vigorous and branching; fragrant salmon-pink blooms. An effective variety that flowers a week earlier than most other floribundas.

'Picasso', 800 mm (2½ ft). Compact and bushy in growth, now more

Left 'Living Fire', a vigorous grower, is a fine bedding variety. Below 'News', introduced in 1969, was the first purple floribunda.

'Lili Marlene', 800 mm (2½ ft). Compact, branching growth, with an ideal habit for bedding; very popular for its scarlet-red flowers.

'Living Fire', 1 m (3 ft). A vigorous, upright grower; freely produced orange flowers, with shades of scarlet and golden yellow. Most effective as a bedding variety.

'Manx Queen', 1 m (3 ft). Compact in growth; its rich gold flowers are flushed with bronze and red.

'Mary Sumner', 1.2 m (4 ft). A very vigorous, tall, and upright grower; slightly fragrant, coppery orange-salmon flowers and handsome, disease-resistant foliage.

'Matangi', 1.1 m (3½ ft). Vigorous, upright grower; slightly fragrant, spectacular vermilion flowers with a white eye and silvery reverse. Free-flowering over a long season.

'Molly McGredy', 1 m (3 ft). A robust, bushy grower; interestingly shaped, very free-flowering blooms of cherry red.

'Moon Maiden', 800 mm (2½ ft). An open, spreading grower; creamy yellow flowers. A variety that associ-

widely known as the 'Hand-Painted Rose'; vari-coloured flowers, usually two shades of cherry red flecked and streaked with silvery white. Produces masses of blooms late into autumn if lightly pruned. Suffers from black spot.

'Pink Parfait', 800 mm (2½ ft). Healthy and upright in growth; prolific, shapely, weather-resistant, light-pink and cream flowers. Excellent for bedding.

'Poppy Flash', 800 mm (2½ ft). Medium in height and vigorous; bright orange-vermilion flowers freely produced.

'Priscilla Burton', 800 mm (2½ ft). A vigorous and branching grower; freely produced, semi-double, wine-red blooms with a silvery eye. Flowers over a long season. Prominent stamens enhance the slightly fragrant flowers.

'Queen Elizabeth', 1.5 m (5 ft). Exceptionally vigorous and apt to over-grow other varieties, so requires careful placing; clear-pink flowers. A well-known and popular variety, good for hedging and useful for cutting.

'Rob Roy', 1 m (3 ft). Fairly tall and vigorous; slightly scented scarlet-crimson flowers, outstanding for colour. Useful also as a cut flower.

'Satchmo', 800 m (2½ ft). Vigorous and bushy, ideal in habit for bedding; a prolific producer of glowing scarlet blooms. Good weather resistance.

'Sea Pearl', 1.1 m (3½ ft). Upright and vigorous in growth; flowers an attractive blend of orange, salmon pink, and peach, nicely formed and scented. Good lasting properties as a cut flower.

'Southampton', 1.2 m (4 ft). A strong upright grower; freely produced, scented, orange-apricot flowers. Disease-resistant to a high degree; ideal for a large bed or hedge, and useful for exhibition.

'Stephen Langdon', 1 m (3 ft). Medium in height but of vigorous growth; freely produced rich crimson-scarlet blooms. In northern England it flowers rather late, so it is unlikely to give a second crop there.

'Sunsilk', 1 m (3 ft). A strong, bushy grower of upright habit; large, shapely, slightly fragrant, lemon-yellow flowers produced in abundance in autumn. Considered by some rosarians to be a hybrid tea variety; good for cutting.

'The Sun', 1.1 m (3½ ft). A tall, healthy grower; slightly scented, salmon-orange flowers.

The fragrant, unfading yellow flowers of 'Korresia', a fine bush rose.

'Trumpeter', 800 mm (2½ ft). A short, compact grower; bright, vermilion-orange or scarlet blooms. Produces abundant flowers throughout the season; healthy in growth and excellent for bedding.

'Vera Dalton', 1.1 m (3½ ft). A vigorous grower; pleasantly scented, soft-pink flowers. Good for bedding.

'Yesterday', 1 m (3 ft). Vigorous and branching in growth, this unusual rose has a charm of its own; sweetly fragrant small flowers opening rose pink, then verging towards lilac. If pruned lightly it will assume the size of a small shrub and fit in very well as a plant for the mixed border.

Dwarf floribundas

The following is a selection of varieties especially suitable for the small garden. They may also be used as edging plants in borders. They should be planted about 500 mm (18 in) apart.

'Baby Bio'. A compact, bushy grower; freely produced golden-yellow flowers which repeat quickly.

'Dicalow' ('Yellow Ribbon'). Compact and bushy in growth; deep golden yellow flowers.

'Dreamland'. Fairly vigorous in growth; attractive, soft peach-pink flowers with a slight fragrance.

'Golden Slippers'. Short and compact in growth; attractive pale gold and orange flowers. A variety which requires and deserves good cultivation.

'Hakuun'. A reliable short grower; white flowers shaded with cream and pink.

'Kim'. An attractive plant, cushion-like in appearance; the yellow flowers flush with red, particularly in autumn.

'Marlena'. Has a compact habit of growth; a mass of crimson-scarlet flowers produced late in the autumn.

'Meteor'. A compact grower; freely produced, brilliant-scarlet flowers.

'Mrs Walter Burns'. A healthy little plant; warm rose-pink flowers.

'Pineapple Poll'. A good bedder; orange-flushed red flowers with a refreshing, spicy fragrance.

'Baby Bio', a dwarf floribunda with rapidly repeating flowers.

'Red Sprite'. A good low-bedding rose; deep-red double flowers.

'Stargazer'. A compact, bushy grower; slightly fragrant, single, bright orange-scarlet flowers.

'Tip Top'. A vigorous, bushy grower; well-formed warm-salmon blooms with shades of pink. Flowers freely over a long season.

'Topsi'. A low grower, ideal for small beds; brilliant orange-scarlet flowers. May require protection against black spot.

'Warrior'. Compact and branching in growth; deep scarlet-red flowers produced in trusses over a long period.

6 Miniature Roses

THE seductive charm of the miniature or 'fairy' roses has made them extremely popular, particularly in the United States, Australia, and New Zealand, and more recently to an increasing extent in Great Britain. Most modern cultivars have been bred from hybrid teas, polyanthas, and floribundas, but they have much smaller leaves and flowers. The great advantage of their size is that they can be grown in situations where there would not be room for other types of roses. People who live in towns can grow miniatures in a window box provided the position is open to some sun; or they can grow them in containers on a balcony or patio.

When they are grown in the garden I prefer them to be in a small area of their own, rather than to see them grown in competition with their more robust cousins. An example of this can be seen in the Royal National Rose Society's gardens at Bone Hill, near St Albans, where a partly sunken garden is devoted to their cultivation.

Almost every type of garden rose grown today owes its origin at least in part to the various species of 'China' rose introduced into Europe from the Far East from the early 19th century onwards. The miniature roses originated from the dwarf form of the China rose, *Rosa chinensis minima*, of which a variety known as 'Roulettii' (sometimes accorded species status as *R. roulettii*) has been used by hybridists. In this form the dwarfing quality is very strong, so that when it is crossed with hybrid teas and floribundas many of the

progeny which result are also small in habit. Two methods of propagation are employed: by cuttings, or by grafting on a suitable understock (*R. multiflora*, being very fibrous rooted, is generally used). Those grown from cuttings are usually sold in pots and produce a dwarf plant. Although regarded by some as more true to character, these have the disadvantage in some

circumstances of a less robust root system, which can make them especially vulnerable in conditions of water shortage. Plants produced by grafting and grown in the open fields of a nursery are sold as bare-rooted plants. They are stronger in growth (too strong for some rosarians, who think they are out of character) and have more resistance to drought.

Miniature roses require the same cultivation as other roses and are subject to the same pests and diseases. Plants can be grown in 100 mm (4 in) or 125 mm (5 in) pots in a compost such as John Innes No. 2; good loamless composts are also suitable. Efficient drainage is essential and should be provided by covering the bottom of the pot with a few small pebbles or similar material. Although very suitable as pot plants, roses are not really happy growing in the home. They may be brought in for some days when in bloom, but they should be put outdoors again afterwards. As they flower over a long season they can, of course, be taken indoors several times during the summer.

Miniature roses are produced for sale mainly by specialists, who also produce miniature standards. Standards are forms in which the development of flowering growths is restricted to the top of a single tall, upright stem. In miniature roses they generally come in two sizes, the smaller stems about 300 mm (12 ins) tall, and the larger ones about 1 m (3 ft) tall. The standards are very attractive in a garden completely devoted to this charming race of roses. Climbing miniatures are also available; they can attain 1.5 m (5 ft) in height when well established, and even more in sheltered positions.

Miniature roses are frequently recommended, because of their size and hardiness, for planting in rock gardens; but this idea is disapproved of,

Above left The vivid blooms of 'Fire Princess'. **Right** An attractive corner of the miniature-rose garden of the RNRS, St Albans.

not surprisingly, by purist alpine-plant enthusiasts. They make very attractive cut flowers, and some people use them with telling effect for desk decoration or in a small room where larger plants would be out of place.

Selection

'Angela Rippon'. Tiny flowers on compact plant; lovely fragrant, salmon-pink blooms.

'Baby Darling', 300 mm (12 in). Salmon-orange flowers.

'Baby Masquerade', 380 mm (15 in). A popular standard; its yellow blooms, flushed with pink and crimson, flower almost throughout the season.

'Bambino', 300 mm (12 in). Perfectly shaped rose-pink flowers.

'Coralin', 450 mm (18 in). Attractive orange-red flowers.

'Darling Flame'. A popular variety; bright-orange flowers with gold shading.

'Dresden Doll', 380 mm (15 in). A miniature moss rose; lovely china-pink, well-mossed buds, and shell-pink flowers with yellow stamens produced throughout the summer.

'Easter Morning', 300 mm (12 in). Its exquisite, double, ivory-white flowers are a little large for the purist but are highly regarded by some growers.

'Eleanor', 300 mm (12 in). An established favourite; small, double, deep coral-pink flowers with a white base.

'Fashion Flame'. Attractive relatively large coral-pink flowers, which resist wet weather.

'Fire Princess'. Fiery scarlet-vermilion flowers.

'Frosty'. Unusual spreading habit; its pale-pink buds open to greenish white flowers with a button eye.

'Gold Coin', 250 mm (10 in). Small, double, buttercup-yellow flowers freely produced.

'Golden Angel'. Golden yellow flowers, rather large for the purist but popular with many growers.

'Gold Pin'. Masses of scented, bright-yellow flowers.

'Green Diamond'. A most unusual variety; its pale-pink flowers change after opening to a soft green.

Above left Doubled-flowered 'Gold Coin'.
Left 'Stacey Sue', popular with exhibitors.

'Gypsy Jewel'. Attractive coral-orange double flowers.

'Judy Fischer'. Delicate pink flowers with an undertone of yellow.

'Kara'. An unusual small, single rose; pink flowers with well-mossed buds.

'Lavender Lace'. Attractive lavender-coloured flowers. Needs watching for black spot.

'Little Flirt'. Orange-red flowers with yellow reverse: a striking combination.

'Magic Carousel', 300 mm (12 in). Pretty double flowers of white-tipped rosy red.

'New Penny', 300 mm (12 in). Bushy; salmon-orange flowers.

'Perla de Montserrat', 300 mm (12 in). A beautiful miniature version of

'Lady Sylvia'; warm rose-pink, paling at the edges. Dainty and shapely in bud.

'Pour Toi', 250 mm (10 in). A popular variety, dainty in growth; the beautifully formed buds open cream, then turn white with a hint of green.

'Rise'n'Shine'. A newcomer from North America; buttercup-yellow flowers.

'Rosina', 300 mm (12 in). Deservedly a favourite owing to its freely produced, classically shaped bright-yellow flowers.

'Scarlet Gem', 250 mm (10 in). A popular variety often grown as a pot plant and also useful as a standard; small, double, scarlet flowers which retain their colour well.

'Old Blush', a long-flowering China rose.

'Stacey Sue'. An attractive, bushy plant; freely produced, small, mid-pink flowers ideal for exhibition.

'Starina', 250 mm (10 in). A very attractive miniature; bi-coloured vivid orange-scarlet and gold flowers.

'Stars'n'Stripes'. A unique variety; double pink blooms with red stripes.

'Sweet Fairy'. A low-growing plant; sweetly perfumed lilac-pink flowers.

'Wee Man', 380 mm (15 in). A very bushy plant; showy crimson-scarlet flowers, a little on the large side for the purist. Must be watched for black spot.

'Yellow Doll', 300 mm (12 in). Soft-yellow flowers with narrow petals.

Climbing Miniatures

'Climbing Jackie'. Up to 1.5 m (5 ft). Produces a heavy crop of soft-yellow to creamy white flowers in spring, with a further display later. The double flowers have some fragrance.

'Climbing Pompon de Paris'. A sport of 'Pompon de Paris' which will attain 1.8 m (6 ft) and more in a sheltered situation; double, rose-pink blooms. It flowers early (May), but later in the season it will develop only a few of its double blooms. Easily propagated from cuttings, it grows exceedingly well on its own roots.

'Nozomi'. 1.5 m (5 ft) or more in good soil. Useful if allowed to grow naturally as a ground-cover plant with spreading, arching growths; single peach-pink flowers produced freely in trusses, but there is little recurrent bloom.

'Pink Cameo'. Up to 1.5 m (5 ft), it produces small, rosy pink flowers throughout the summer. Although classified as a climbing miniature, it is shrub-like in growth, standing well without support.

China Roses

This name is now given to varieties of the older species of China rose.

'Cécile Brunner', 600 mm (2 ft). This is the 'Sweetheart Rose', almost a century old; numerous scented, pale bluish-pink blooms, perfect in form, recurrent in flowering. Thimble-like in size, the flowers look delightful in miniature arrangements when cut. It is now more familiar in its climbing form for garden display.

'Little White Pet', 600 mm (2 ft). Not a true China, but it deserves a place in this section. Beautifully formed creamy white rosette blooms, very free blooming, it is seldom without some flowers during the season.

'Mutablis', 1.1 m (3½ ft). Can grow taller, especially in a warm, sheltered garden; single, pale-copper flowers which change colour as they mature to pink and finally to coppery crimson. Very free flowering over a long season. Thrives against a wall.

'Old Blush', 1 to 1.2 m (3 to 4 ft). A well-known variety often called the 'monthly rose', probably because of its free-flowering habit; semi-double, rosy pink flowers. Supposed to be the inspiration of Thomas Moore's poem 'The Last Rose of Summer' – a tribute to its long flowering season. Easily grown from cuttings.

'Perle d'Or', 1 m (3 ft). A dwarf shrub, resembling 'Cecile Brunner' (see above) but with larger flowers; buff-apricot blooms. Lovely for miniature-flower arrangements; has a beautiful scent.

Left The fully double flowers of 'Starina' are beautifully set off by glossy foliage.

Right The bicoloured 'Darling Flame' is one of the most popular miniature roses.

7 Rose Species and Near Hybrids

Most roses that one sees, either in formal displays or in suburban gardens, are varieties based on fairly recently categorized types – hybrid tea, floribunda, miniature and so on. These varieties have beautiful form and colour and, most important, recurrent flowering – often throughout the season.

Species roses – descendants of wild roses growing in many parts of the world – have a charm and beauty all their own. Most of them flower only once a season, but many provide autumn colour in the form of hips. They are easy to cultivate, thriving in most well-drained soils that are not acid. Young plants may require some pruning in the first few years to give them shape, especially those that produce hips. The best flowers and hips develop on strong growths formed the previous year.

Selection

Rosa × andersonii, 2 m (6 ft). A chance hybrid of *R. canina*, the dog rose; a very showy, single, brilliant pink flower with a golden centre.

R. banksiae lutea, up to 9 m (30 ft). The well-known Yellow Banksian rose, which requires and deserves a warm wall; small, double, scented, butter-yellow flowers. Prune only old wood or surplus wood after flowering.

R. californica plena, up to 2.4 m (8 ft) on good soil; deep-pink, pleasantly scented flowers in mid-summer.

R. ecae, 1.5 m (5 ft). A rare shrub of dainty appearance, which appreciates a warm wall; brilliant, 25 mm (1 in) wide, single, golden yellow flowers in May.

R. farreri persetosa, 1.5 m (5 ft). The 'threepenny-bit rose', a very graceful shrub with arching branches of delicate growth; tiny leaves and soft pink flowers, coral red in bud, followed by small hips.

R. fedtschenkoana, 2.4 m (8 ft). A large shrub rose with distinctive, greyish foliage; single, white flowers produced continuously during the summer, followed by bright red hips.

R. forrestiana, 2 m (6 ft). A medium-sized shrub with arching growths; freely produced, single, rosy crimson flowers, followed by scarlet hips.

R. × highdownensis, 3 m (10 ft). A hybrid from *R. moyesii*, prized mainly for its beautiful, flask-shaped, orange-red hips; single, deep-pink flowers.

R. holodonta, 3 m (10 ft). Closely related to *R. moyesii*, but slightly less vigorous; remarkable hips, 60 mm (2¼ in) long, flask-shaped, and orange-red, produced in great abundance.

R. hugonis, 2 m (6 ft). An early flowering shrub with delicate fern-like foliage; single, pale creamy yellow flowers in late May and early June.

R. moyesii, 3 m (10 ft). A vigorous shrub; single, deep blood-red flowers and dainty foliage. Splendid flask-shaped hips, 40 mm (1½ in) long, and persistent for nearly three months from late August.

R. moyesii 'Geranium'. At 2.1 m (7 ft), it is more compact than *R. moyesii*, but with more brilliant flowers and more spectacular hips.

R. primula, up to 2.4 m (8 ft). The incense rose; single, creamy yellow flowers, usually in May. Chiefly distinguished for the scent of incense from its delicate foliage.

R. × pteragonis 'Cantabrigiensis' 2.7 m (9 ft). A lovely rose; single, creamy yellow flowers in late May or early June.

R. rubrifolia, 2.1 m (7 ft). A vigorous shrub with lovely glaucous, purple-grey foliage much used by flower arrangers.

R. sericea pteracantha, 2.4 m (8 ft). Will attain this height if left to grow naturally, but less if pruned hard to encourage young growths, which are notable for their large, triangular, translucent, blood-red thorns; single, white flowers with only four petals.

R. setipoda, 2.1 m (7 ft). A handsome arching shrub with sweet-briar-scented foliage; single, purplish pink flowers.

R. sweginzowii, 3 m (10 ft) high and wide. A vigorous shrub somewhat akin to *R. moyesii*; single, bright rose-pink flowers; bristly orange-red hips.

R. virginiana, 1.5 m (5 ft). A dense-growing shrub; single, bright, deep-pink flowers. Its foliage turns fiery orange-red and deep yellow.

R. willmottiae, 1.8 m (6 ft). An arching, graceful shrub with attractive fern-like foliage; single, pale-pink flowers; small orange-red hips.

R. woodsii fendleri, 1.5 m (5 ft). A rose grown mainly for its scarlet hips, which persist through autumn; fragrant, single, lilac-pink flowers.

Rosa moyesii 'Geranium', probably the best hybrid of this species for the smaller garden.

8 Shrub Roses

No rose garden of any size is really complete without some shrub roses, and they are particularly valuable in large gardens. The name is somewhat misleading since botanically speaking all roses are shrubs. The modern types known as shrub roses are mainly hybrids and cultivars of the old species roses. They make splendid garden shrubs in their own right, and have always been much admired, not only by horticulturists but also by artists.

Older shrub roses

I will begin with the white roses derived from *Rosa alba* because I have long and happily nostalgic memories of them and because they have many virtues. They are hardy, vigorous, and long-lived, as they have been for three centuries. They have lovely greyish foliage, and a refreshing scent.

Rosa alba maxima, 2.4 m (8 ft), the Great Double White or Jacobite rose. A shrub of great vigour which grows well all over the United Kingdom. It is useful for north-facing walls as well as in a large border. The beautiful creamy white flowers have just a hint of buff in the petal folds. It flowers freely in June but is not recurrent.

R. alba semi-plena. Even more vigorous than *R. alba maxima*, it is generally considered to be the original white rose of the House of York. The semi-double white flowers are freely borne in clusters and have good hips in autumn.

The following are a few of the many fine decorative varieties of shrub roses.

'Céleste' (also known as 'Celestial'). A shrub of considerable vigour up to 2 m (6 ft) in height and width. It is particularly attractive when the flowers are opening, and is a great favourite with admirers of old roses. The delicacy of its clear-pink flowers combines perfectly with the grey-green foliage. It is sometimes called the Minden rose.

'Félicité Parmentier'. Reaches to about 1.2 m (4 ft) but is of less-upright habit than others in this group. The rich cream tone of the buds vanishes as they open to exquisite flowers of blush pink. When fully open the flowers are beautifully set off by the grey-green leaves.

'Great Maiden's Blush', 1.5 m (5 ft). Ranks high among shrub roses. It has been a familiar sight in cottage gardens for several hundred years and is especially attractive as an informal hedge. The attractively scented blush-pink flowers fade at the edges as they open but retain this colour at the centre. The grey-green leaves are a perfect foil to the exquisite colour of the blooms.

'Königin von Dänemark' (Queen of Denmark). A popular shrub of medium vigour which can reach 1.8 m (6 ft); it originated as a seedling from 'Great Maiden's Blush'. The double flowers are vivid cerise-pink when half open and reflex to a soft, warm pink. The blooms show a button centre, are fragrant, and are offset by lead-grey foliage.

'Mme Legras de St Germain', 1.8 m (6 ft). An *R. alba* hybrid with fully double, glistening white blooms with a rich-cream centre. The vigorous growths are almost thornless and have pale green leaves.

'Mme Plantier'. Possibly of *R. alba* parentage, although sometimes regarded as a *noisette* rose (a type established originally by the crossing of China and Western species by the French nurseryman Philippe Noisette). It generally grows as a sprawling bush 1.2 m (4 ft) in height and width. The dainty foliage can hardly be seen when the very double, flat, creamy white flowers are in their full glory. These show a green button centre and have a rich, sweet fragrance which carries freely in the air.

Above left 'Mme Hardy', a lovely damask rose. **Right** 'Celestial' (or 'Céleste'), an old shrub rose.

Old garden roses

The old garden species and their varieties do not as a rule require much pruning. When flowering is over some of the old growths should be removed, and this will encourage strong basal growths which can be cut back by a

This will result in fewer but better flowers and the plants as a whole will be more compact.

Damask Roses

R. damascena, the damask rose, is so-called owing to the tradition that Crusaders introduced it to Europe from Damascus. Its fragrance is celebrated and some varieties are used for making

'Mme Pierre Oger', one of the most popular of the Bourbon roses.

third to lessen wind damage. The albas in particular put up with some neglect and need pruning only occasionally. Most gallicas (derivatives of the ancient *R. gallica*, the French red rose) are naturally compact. Centifolias, damasks, and moss roses can have side shoots shortened to two or three buds in February, and new growths can be reduced to one third of their length.

the scent known as attar of roses. The following are popular varieties.

'Celsiana', 1.5 m (5 ft). This beautiful old rose, known for more than 200 years, is a graceful shrub with grey-green, scented foliage. The large, fragrant, semi-double flowers are pro-

duced in clusters of bright dog-rose pink, fading to blush-pink.

'Ispahan', 1.5 m (5 ft). A vigorous upright grower which makes a valuable garden plant because of its good growth and long flowering season. A clear, warm, rose-pink in colour, the blooms last well when cut.

'Kazanluk', 1.8 m (6 ft). A variety which takes its name from the Bulgarian town and district where this rose is used for the production of attar of roses. The full, heavily quartered blooms are rich rose-pink and have a glorious perfume.

'Mme Hardy', 1.8 m (6 ft). A rose of superb beauty, regarded by many lovers of old roses as having no peer. The flowers, which open creamy white, become pure white with a green eye. With its profusion of dark green leaves and the fresh lemon scent of its flowers, it should have a place in any collection of old garden roses.

'Versicolor', 1.5 m (5 ft). An interesting rose, known traditionally by many as the 'York and Lancaster', it requires good soil and cool conditions. The flowers are bluish white and light pink, sometimes either one colour or the other, and sometimes parti-coloured. It is often confused with the well-known striped sport of *Rosa gallica officinalis*, also called 'Versicolor', which in my view is a much more useful garden plant.

Bourbon Roses

The Bourbons were derived in the 19th century from crosses between the China and damask roses. In appearance they are like vigorous 'old' roses and retain much of their floral charm.

'Boule de Neige', 1.5 m (5 ft). A vigorous erect shrub, with rich, double, scented, creamy white flowers which reflex into a ball shape. Recurrent flowering during the summer. One of the best roses in this group.

'Commandant Beaurepaire', 1.5 m (5 ft). A free-flowering shrub, it is apt to make a thick bush, so it requires careful pruning. The large double flowers of deep purple-crimson are streaked with lighter pink, but are rather variable. When in full bloom in late June this is one of the most spectacular of striped roses.

'Gipsy Boy' (Zigeuner Knabe), 2 m (6 ft) or more. A very vigorous shrub or pillar rose which can be allowed to grow up an old tree for support. The semi-double flowers are a bright purple-crimson that deepens as they mature. Freely produced but no recurrent bloom. Large orange-red hips follow. Extremely thorny.

'Honorine de Brabant', 2 m (6 ft). A fine vigorous shrub. The loosely cupped blooms are pale pink splashed irregularly with purplish crimson. Seldom out of flower and fruitily scented.

'La Reine Victoria', 2 m (6 ft). A shrub of erect, narrow growth and medium vigour, continuously in flower during the season. The blooms are renowned for their exquisite cup-like shape, rich fragrance, and warm rose pink colouring. May suffer from black spot. This variety has achieved fame as the parent of 'Mme Pierre Oger'.

'Louise Odier', 2 m (6 ft). A vigorous, branching shrub which recurrently produces its double, round flowers of soft, warm pink in profusion. A valuable rose with old-world perfection of form, beautiful fragrance, good foliage, and a continuous succession of flowers.

'Mme Isaac Pereire', 2.4 m (8 ft). A vigorous shrub suitable for training to a pillar or a wall. The very large, full-double flowers are deep rose-pink with purple shades and are renowned for their fragrance. The blooms are produced in intermittent bursts, and are particularly fine in autumn. A most effective garden plant.

'Mme Lauriol de Barny', 1.5 m (5 ft) or more. This is one of the finest of the Bourbon group. The large, double flowers of silvery, pale purplish pink are quartered when fully open and have a strong, fruity scent. It does not recur much, but compensates by the richness and abundance of its main performance.

'Mme Pierre Oger', 1.5 m (5 ft). This popular favourite originated in 1878 as a silvery pink sport of 'La Reine Victoria'. Its colour varies somewhat according to the weather, but it has all the good qualities of its parent, a rich fragrance, and a dainty form.

'Souvenir de la Malmaison', 3 m (10 ft). A vigorous shrub which requires the support of a pillar; the bush form is seldom seen. The large blooms are pale blush pink, fading as they age and becoming flat and quartered. Very fragrant. Generally produced in two crops beginning about midsummer,

with flowers of better quality in September.

'Variegata di Bologna', 1.5 m (5 ft). A vigorous shrub if grown in good soil. The rounded, somewhat globular flowers are white, neatly striped with carmine-purple. Recurrent in bloom and free enough to create a spectacle. It may require protection against black spot.

Rosa gallica 'Versicolor' (known also as 'Rosa Mundi') is more than 400 years old.

'Zéphirine Drouhin', 3 m (10 ft). A vigorous shrub which can be allowed to grow naturally as a climber or, if pruned heavily, as a shrub or hedge. Possibly the most familiar of the Bourbons, it is popularly known as the Thornless Rose. The semi-double flowers are bright cerise-carmine and have a strong fruity fragrance. Very free flowering and continuous if dead-headed frequently. (A sport, 'Kathleen Harrap', appeals to some rosarians because of its pleasing light pink flowers, but it lacks vigour.) Somewhat susceptible to mildew and black spot.

Gallicas

Rosa gallica, the French red rose, has had much to do with the ancestry of our modern garden roses. In the 18th century the gallicas were used in breeding by the Dutch and later by the French, and its many offspring became very popular in the 19th century as garden plants.

'Belle de Crécy', 1.2 m (4 ft). An untidy shrub which is almost thornless. The flowers are rich pink in the opening stage, maturing to soft violet. Regarded highly by some, its habit does not appeal to others. Good cultivation to prevent drying out is especially helpful with this variety.

'Camaieux', 1 m (3 ft). A short shrub with unique appeal: on opening, the bluish-white petals are liberally striped and splashed with light crimson, flushing to violet purple, and eventually fading to violet grey. Sage green leaves help to make this one of the most distinctive of the old striped roses.

'Cardinal de Richelieu', 1.2 m (4 ft) or more. Of medium vigour and few thorns. Very free flowering, with its blooms opening as a sumptuous purple, then fading to Parma violet. The

Right 'Frau Dagmar Hartopp', a rugosa, with hips. **Below** 'Complicata', a gallica.

ball-like flowers as they reflex assume colours akin to those of black grapes. Must be grown well and fed generously, and much of the old flowering wood must be pruned away.

'Charles de Mills', 1.5 m (5 ft). One of the best gallicas for general garden purposes, it has large, flat, quartered blooms which are very full and sweetly scented. Colouring is opulent crimson-purple through maroon to wine shades.

'Complicata'. Although of unknown origin, this variety is sometimes grouped with the gallica roses. Will attain 2.4 m (8 ft) if given the support of a small tree (I have done this in my own garden). The large, single, pink flowers with a white centre are like those of a deeper-coloured and enlarged dog rose (*R. canina*), which may claim a share in its ancestry. Good on light soils and easily rooted from

cuttings. Where space is available this is one of the finest of single roses and a first-class garden plant.

'Duchesse de Montebello', 1.5 m (5 ft) when given good cultivation. Produces sprays 1 m (3 ft) long of small cup-shaped shell-pink flowers which are good for cutting. Early flowering and almost thornless, it probably derives part of its ancestry from the albas.

'Jenny Duval', 1.1 m (3½ ft). A shrub of medium vigour with blooms of spectacular colours – cerise, magenta, and violet in the centre, shading to lilac white. Very shapely buds. Exquisite at all stages.

Rosa gallica officinalis, 1.2 m (4 ft). The Apothecary's Rose, generally considered to be the red rose of the House of Lancaster. A shrub of medium vigour, it is inclined to sucker (develop underground basal shoots) if on its own

roots, growing into small thickets. The semi-double flowers are light crimson with yellow stamens. A good garden shrub, and one of the oldest in cultivation.

'Tuscany', 1.2 m (4 ft). Known also as 'Old Velvet' owing to the texture of its petals, this is a plant of bushy growth which suckers in light soils if on its own roots. The semi-double flowers are rich crimson-maroon with hints of purple offset by yellow stamens.

'Tuscany Superb'. Possibly a sport from 'Tuscany', it is more sumptuous than the latter, with larger, fuller flowers that tend to conceal the attractive stamens.

'Versicolor'. A sport from *R. gallica officinalis* (see page 46), it was first recorded in the 16th century and is often found in old gardens; known

also as the 'Rosa Mundi', it is often confused with the York and Lancaster 'Versicolor'. The flowers are striped pale pink and white, very gaudy in appearance. It makes a spectacular low hedge. Sometimes susceptible to mildew in autumn.

Centifolias

The cabbage rose, or Provence rose, beloved of our great grandparents and long popular in English gardens, is not a wild species but a complex hybrid, presumably of garden origin. Dutch breeders began to take an interest in centifolias (as they are now called) in about 1580 and persevered for over a century to attain perfection. Their full, globular flowers on gracefully curving stems appear in many of the flower paintings of the old Dutch masters.

'Bullata', 1.5 m (5 ft). A shrub of botanical and historical interest, with large, rich-pink, cup-shaped flowers, beautifully scented. Remarkable for its enormous crinkled leaves, deeply tinted with mahogany and bearing a strong resemblance to 'Continuity' lettuce.

'Cristata', 1.2 m (4 ft). Also called 'Crested Moss', it is not in fact regarded as a true moss rose. The crested wings of the calyx give the buds some resemblance to a three-cornered cockaded hat, giving rise to its other name, 'Chapeau de Napoléon'. The soft rose-pink flowers are fully double.

'De Meaux', 1 m (3 ft). A neat, erect dwarf shrub of considerable charm which makes an attractive small hedge. The pompon-like flowers, which open from lovely buds in great profusion, are rose pink and sweetly scented. A form 'White de Meaux' is white with pink-centred flowers.

'Fantin-Latour', 1.5 m (5 ft). A favourite shrub rose. Vigorous and free-blooming, the double flowers are pale pink, shaded rich blush, and are cup shaped. A beautifully fragrant rose full of old-world charm.

'La Noblesse', 1.2 m (4 ft). A superb shrub with gloriously scented flowers of warm, deep rose. Continues to flower when many of the other 'old' roses have finished.

'Tour de Malakoff', 2 m (6 ft). A large shrub inclined to be untidy in habit except on good fertile soil. The large, loosely double flowers, mauve-

Fragrant 'Fantin-Latour', a popular centifolia.

pink with purple shades, change later to Parma violet and grey lavender. Very floriferous but not recurrent, it is often used as a pillar rose.

Moss Roses

Rosa centifolia muscosa (moss rose), 1.2 m (4 ft). This rose created a great stir early in the 18th century when it was introduced from the Continent. An attractive sport from the cabbage rose, it came into its heyday in the 19th century, when it featured in the garden of almost every self-respecting rose grower. The clear-pink flowers are scented and the buds are well mossed. A shrub of medium vigour and of considerable charm.

'Alfred de Dalmas' (also known as 'Mousseline'). A compact shrub about 1.2 m (4 ft) high. The large, very free-flowering, cup-shaped blooms are delicate flesh pink in colour and are produced throughout the summer. Furnished with brownish green moss.

'General Kleber', up to 1.2 m (4 ft). A compact, vigorous shrub; its large, double flowers, open, flat, and quartered, are a soft, pure pink and richly scented. It is well furnished with greenish brown moss.

'Henri Martin', 1.5 m (5 ft) or more. A vigorous shrub which flowers profusely. The non-recurrent large, light-crimson flowers are produced in clusters that make a fine contrast with their green moss.

'Jeanne de Montfort', 2 m (6 ft). A tall, robust shrub which requires a good deal of space. Clear, warm-pink flowers which fade to blush pink are freely produced in large clusters. The buds are well mossed in a brownish tone.

'Little Gem', 600 mm (2 ft). A charming miniature with flowers of light crimson, opening to flat pompon blooms.

'Maréchal Davoust', up to 1.5 m (5 ft). A good shrub with perfectly shaped buds with brownish moss. The large, saucer-shaped flowers in shades of lilac and mauve with flashes of carmine are prodigally produced and make a splendid display.

'Nuits de Young', 1.2 m (4 ft). A thin, somewhat sparse shrub but distinctive because of its unusual dark-

Above right 'William Lobb', a fine moss rose.
Right 'Ferdinand Pichard', a popular, bushy hybrid perpetual.

purple or maroon colour, with dark, brownish red moss. One of the most famous of the moss roses.

'William Lobb', 1.8 m (6 ft) or more. A very vigorous, free-flowering shrub producing scented, dark purplish crimson flowers fading to pale purplish lavender. Buds and pedicels (the short stalks connecting the flower with the main stem) are well covered with green moss. Also known as the 'old velvet moss'.

Hybrid Perpetuals

The hybrid perpetual roses were the popular bedding roses of the 19th century until they were replaced by the hybrid teas. Many are too tall by present-day standards; but they can be pegged down, when they will produce

The double flower of 'Vick's Caprice', a hybrid perpetual from North America.

flowers along their entire length and give an attractive display. They are more effective as border plants unless there is room for large beds. They flower recurrently. Pruning should be carried out in February or March, cutting away old twiggy growths and shortening other growths by a third of their length.

'Baron Girod de l'Ain'. A vigorous shrub about 1.5 m (5 ft) high; large, recurrent, double, dark crimson-red flowers edged with white, and scented.

'Empereur du Maroc'. A short shrub, usually under 1.2 m (4 ft); double flowers of deep crimson-red, strongly scented and slightly quartered.

'Ferdinand Pichard', 1.5 m (5 ft). A valuable rose because of its recurrent flowering; medium-sized pink flowers, heavily streaked and splashed with crimson.

'Frau Karl Druschki', 1.8 m (6 ft) if lightly pruned. A famous rose, introduced in 1901, which still retains its popularity. Regarded by many rosarians as the best white rose, but unfortunately it is scentless. Flowers freely over a long period. Sometimes requires protection against mildew.

'Hugh Dickson'. A red rose famous for its lovely perfume. May be pegged down, as it is a tall grower, and it will then flower freely in summer and again later.

'Mrs John Laing'. A vigorous shrub, 1.5 m (5 ft) and more; strongly scented, cup-shaped, rose-pink flowers. Generally regarded as one of the best of this group, it is sometimes grown as a pot plant. The flowers have good stems and are excellent for cutting.

'Paul Neyron'. A vigorous shrub which may attain 1.8 m (6 ft); enormous, peony-like, deep rose-pink flowers, quartered when fully open.

'Reine des Violettes'. A vigorous shrub sometimes reaching 1.8 m (6 ft); double, quartered flowers open flat and are deep violet purple fading to lilac. Deeply scented.

'Roger Lambelin', 1.2 m (4 ft). A shrub which requires good cultivation to produce its highly distinctive flowers. These are full petalled, deep crimson-red with white edges sometimes extending into the flower, and are fragrant.

'Souvenir du Docteur Jamain'. A shrub of medium vigour about 1.8 m (6 ft), but worth a place on a wall for its well-formed, richly fragrant, deep purplish crimson flowers; bears large orange-red hips. Old growths must be removed when they have finished flowering.

'Ulrich Brunner Fils'. A shrub of considerable vigour producing 1.8 m (6 ft) growths which flower freely if pegged down near the tips; the scented, bright carmine-red flowers are apt to clash with others, so the plant is most effective when grown on its own.

'Vick's Caprice'. Generally under 1.2 m (4 ft), and of medium vigour; large recurrent, double flowers, rose pink with various stripes and flecks of white and carmine pink.

'Dorothy Wheatcroft', a recurrent modern shrub rose of floribunda type.

Modern shrub roses

This group is becoming increasingly popular for the more informal situations. Most varieties are of bushy habit, and many will attain a height and spread of more than 2 m (6 ft). For convenience in planning, I have divided the selection into recurrent and non-recurrent types.

Recurrent Type

These are especially useful because they provide ornamental value over a long flowering season. Many of them can be used effectively as single specimen shrubs, but they are equally effective for informal hedges. Generally little pruning is required, but the prompt removal of old flowering heads will encourage the plants to flower again. Some varieties are moderate in growth and, although classified as shrubs, can be pruned to grow as large floribundas; as such they are ideal for large beds, and are widely used in public gardens.

'Angelina', 1.2 m (4 ft). A moderate grower with a long flowering season; semi-double, light carmine-pink flowers with a slight fragrance.

'Ballerina'. Moderate in height but of vigorous growth, a useful general-purpose rose for mixed borders, hedges, large beds, or even as a standard; large clusters of small, single, pink flowers; abundant glossy foliage.

'Buff Beauty'. A Pemberton musk of medium height and spreading habit; freely produced, very fragrant apricot-yellow flowers that pale at the edges.

'Chinatown'. A handsome plant of 1.5 m (5 ft) or more; fragrant, double, deep-yellow flowers, sometimes flushed with red.

'Cornelia', 1.5 m (5 ft). A Pemberton musk, spreading and bushy in habit; freely produced apricot-pink flowers intensify in colour in autumn.

'Dorothy Wheatcroft', 1.5 m (5 ft). A tall-growing floribunda-type; brilliant red flowers produced in huge trusses on long growths, particularly in autumn. Effective if planted *en masse*.

'Elmshorn', 1.8 m (6 ft). A vigorous shrub; freely produced cherry-red flowers over a lengthy period.

'Fountain', 1.5 m (5 ft). A medium-growing shrub; blood-red double flowers of hybrid-tea shape borne freely in clusters.

'Frank Naylor', 1.2 m (4 ft). A compact, dense-growing shrub with beautiful foliage, particularly in spring; lightly scented, single, deep crimson-maroon blooms with a golden zone. Needs protection from black spot.

'Fred Loads'. A vigorous shrub which can attain 2.1 m (7 ft) if conditions are good; single, light-vermilion flowers borne in large clusters and very showy. Good for the back of borders, and popular with exhibitors of floribunda roses.

'Goldbonnet'. An effective shrub of 1.2 m (4 ft) and more; abundant bright-yellow flowers.

'Golden Wings'. A vigorous shrub which when pruned hard will reach 1.2 m (4 ft); large, single, light prim-rose-yellow flowers, sweetly scented and produced almost continuously over a long period. Orange-yellow hips follow in autumn. A most attract-ive and beautiful shrub.

'Joseph's Coat', 1.8 m (6 ft) or more. A vigorous grower which, if severely pruned, can be used for large beds and, if lightly pruned, as a specimen shrub or as a climber; freely produced yellow flowers flushed with orange and red, especially effective in autumn.

'Kathleen Ferrier', 1.5 m (5 ft). Medium-growing floribunda-type shrub; strongly scented salmon-pink flowers borne in loose clusters.

'Lavender Lassie', 1.5 m (5 ft). A floribunda-type shrub of medium vig-our; very fragrant, pink-shaded laven-der flowers.

'Magenta', 1.2 m (4 ft). A flori-bunda-type, open and somewhat sprawling in habit; freely produced, beautifully scented variable-coloured flowers, pinkish-lilac to soft deepish mauve.

'Marguerite Hilling'. A vigorous sport of 'Nevada' (see below) which will attain at least 1.5 m (5 ft) in height and width; semi-double, light pink flowers with deeper shading, produced in abundance in June and July but more frugally later in the season. Identical to its parent except in colour.

'Marjorie Fair', 1.2 m (4 ft). Vigor-ous and bushy in growth; single, bright reddish-carmine flowers with a silver

Two recurrent modern shrub roses: **above right** 'Joseph's Coat'; **right** 'Nevada'.

eye. A variety which is much appreciated because of the wealth of colour it produces over a long period.

'Moonlight', 1.5 m (5 ft) and more. Appropriately named, this Pemberton rose is much favoured by those who enjoy their gardens in late evening; semi-double, lemon-cream flowers, with golden stamens and musk scent. If unpruned this variety will scramble over hedges or into small trees.

'Morgensonne' (Morning Sun). A vigorous floribunda-type shrub; beautiful, full golden-yellow flowers.

'Nevada'. One of the finest shrub roses, from 1.5 to 2.4 m (5 to 8 ft) in height and width; large creamy white flowers festoon its arching branches in June and make a lesser display later in the season. Ideal as a single specimen.

'Nymphenburg'. A shrub of up-

right habit and medium growth; delightful salmon-pink, scented flowers.

'Penelope'. Usually about 1.5 m (5 ft) in height and width, and one of the most outstanding Pemberton roses for hedges and borders; freely produced, richly fragrant, pale salmon-pink flowers tinged with apricot, particularly good in autumn. Sometimes shows a tendency to mildew in autumn.

'Poulsen's Park Rose'. A fairly large spreading shrub, 1.5 m (5 ft) and more; abundant large, shapely, silvery pink blooms. Very fragrant.

'Rainbow'. A medium-sized shrub; very freely produced multi-shaded blooms of coral, orange, yellow, and salmon.

'Saga', 1.2 m (4 ft). An upright, bushy grower of floribunda type;

lovely semi-double, white flowers with shades of buff which deepen in autumn.

'The Fairy', 1 m (3 ft). A spreading grower included here as a low shrub as it does not conform in type to modern floribunda roses; small, double, soft-pink flowers produced in great abundance after a late start. Best planted either in a bed or in a mixed border, where it will excel most of its neighbours.

'Will Scarlet', up to 1.8 m (6 ft). A strong, bushy shrub; slightly scented, semi-double, hunting-pink flowers produced over a lengthy period. The good display of fine orange-red hips in late autumn and winter is a pleasant bonus.

'Raubritter', a non-recurrent modern shrub rose, is useful for ground cover.

Non-recurrent Type

The following is a list of varieties that are essentially non-recurrent (although some have a few late-season flowers), and are valued particularly for their early-summer blooms. Several of them produce hips in autumn.

'Canary Bird', up to 2.1 m (7 ft) in good soil conditions. A deservedly popular hybrid from *R. xanthina*, it is one of the first roses to flower in May; single canary-yellow flowers, borne in great profusion and beautifully set off by grey-green, ferny foliage.

'Cerise Bouquet', 1.8 m (6 ft) and more. A distinctive shrub; small, greyish foliage offsets the semi-double, cerise-crimson flowers produced on long, arching sprays.

'Constance Spry'. A hefty grower

of 1.8 m (6 ft) and more in height and width; distinctively fragrant, somewhat cupped, soft-pink flowers borne with great freedom.

'Fritz Nobis', 1.5 m (5 ft), possibly more on good soil, and vigorous in growth; beautifully shaped buds, and fragrant, semi-double, pale salmon-pink flowers. Bears dark-red hips which persist for a long time. A most valuable shrub.

'Frühlingsgold' (Spring Gold), 2.1 m (7 ft). A tall shrub which does well on most soils; large, creamy yellow flowers, slightly semi-double, tending to fade a little, but with a rich fragrance which carries for some distance. Given sufficient space, it is a first-class shrub.

'Frühlingsmorgen (Spring Morning), 1.5 m (5 ft) and more on good soil; beautifully formed, single, clear rose-pink flowers with a yellow centre, whose purple-maroon stamens add to their beauty.

'Golden Chersonese', 1.8 m (6 ft). An upright-growing shrub with slender, arching growths; beautifully fragrant, single, deep buttercup-yellow flowers. Worth trying as a hedge, it seems most at home when it is not too exposed to cold winds.

'Max Graf'. A trailing rose, the result of crossing *R. rugosa* with *R. wichuraiana*; abundant masses of single, pink flowers which lighten towards the base. Generally planted for ground cover, 1.5 m (5 ft) apart, for which purpose it is admirably suited.

'Raubritter'. A sprawling shrub, useful for ground cover or for covering banks, where eventually it will extend to 1.8 m (6 ft) across, or even more in good soil; slightly scented, semi-double, light-pink flowers freely borne in clusters, and delightfully incurled into globular blooms of great charm. Some protection against mildew may be required.

'Scharlachglut' (better known as 'Scarlet Fire'). A great arching shrub up to 2.4 m (8 ft) on good soil. Although non-recurrent, it flowers over a longish period; large, single, beautifully shaped scarlet-crimson blooms borne freely all along the branches. Large, pear-shaped, orange-scarlet hips which last for a considerable time add greatly to the value of this fine shrub, which is especially effective if trained up a wall.

Ground-cover roses

Much is heard these days about ground-cover plants. That roses have a contribution to make here can be seen in the Display Garden of the RNRS at St Albans, where a large bed has been set aside for varieties suitable for this purpose. The following is a typical selection.

scarlet-crimson. Its single deep-pink flowers are produced in June and July. A very good plant for growing and filling in spaces at the front of a rose border.

R. wichuraiana. A naturally prostrate grower which, if it is in the right place, will make young growths up to 3 m (10 ft) long during the season. Very attractive glossy, semi-evergreen foliage. The scented, single, white flowers are attractive and are produced

(1 ft) from the ground. It has become well established as a ground-cover plant, rooting as it grows. The single, bright-pink flowers with good yellow stamens are like a much-improved dog rose. Scented, with attractive glossy foliage.

'Nozomi'. If allowed to grow naturally, it produces low, arching growths about 450 mm (1½ ft) from the ground and covering 1.2 m (4 ft). The small, single, non-recurrent flowers are pro-

Rosa × paulii 'Rosea', a fragrant cultivar, is an excellent type for ground cover.

Rosa kordesii. This has been given the status of a species, although it arose in cultivation as a seedling from 'Max Graf' (a hybrid which is generally sterile). It can be grown as a low climber, but if allowed to sprawl naturally it is useful as ground cover. Produces semi-double, deep-pink flowers over a considerable period but is not recurrent.

R. nitida, 600 mm (2 ft). A dwarf shrub which suckers freely but takes time to establish itself. It is striking in autumn when its foliage turns deep

late, usually after mid-July.

'Temple Bells'. A newcomer from America, very similar to *R. wichuraiana* in habit and lateness of flowering, and possibly even more vigorous. The white flowers have very pronounced yellow stamens and are fragrant. It roots freely along the ground.

'Lady Curzon'. A hybrid, derived from *R. rugosa,* which will cover an area 2.4 m (8 ft) square, making a large, prickly mound. Attractive, with good foliage and large, single, pale-pink flowers. Scented, but not recurrent.

'Max Graf'. A trailing shrub which generally does not rise above 300 mm

duced freely in trusses and are pale pearly pink in colour. The glossy foliage is attractive.

R. × paulii. A trailer most suitable for fairly large gardens where it will form an impenetrable mound 1 m (3 ft) high and at least 1.8 m (6 ft) across. Produces liberally its single, slightly starry white flowers, which are delicately scented. Excessively thorny.

R. × paulii 'Rosea'. Possibly a sport of *R. × paulii,* but much reduced in vigour and consequently a much better garden plant. It produces particularly beautiful fragrant, single, deep-pink flowers with white centres and with a mass of golden stamens.

9 Ramblers and Climbers

IN general, ramblers have a spreading habit of growth, but can usually be trained up low garden features; climbers are sturdier and have a more upright habit, and are suitable for training up tall fences and walls. In their cultivated form, the rambler and climber roses can be collectively divided into two types. The more recent, which are nowadays far more popular in smaller gardens, are of relatively moderate growth; most of them have a prolonged period of flowering and many (notably the Kordes varieties) are recurrent. The second type are the older ramblers and climbers, which are very vigorous in growth, require much pruning, but are still very useful for training up the taller garden structures.

Moderate growers

These, if pruned by cutting back strong growths, make fine, spreading plants. They are ideal for screens, pillars, walls, fences, and trellises, but are not tall enough for arches or pergolas.

'Aloha', 1.5 to 3 m (5 to 10 ft). Can be grown as a shrub, but with good cultivation builds up into a fine pillar rose, and succeeds on north-facing walls; scented, double, hybrid-tea-type blooms, deep pink in centre and paling towards edges with a suffusion of orange.

'Altissimo', 1.8 to 2.4 m (6 to 8 ft). A vigorous and healthy favourite with those who love singles; non-scented, freely produced, large, velvety, blood-red blooms shaded with crimson and with bright golden stamens. Makes a fine shrub if main stems are shortened.

'Bantry Bay', 3 m (10 ft). A vigorous grower; freely produced semi-double, light rose-pink flowers throughout the season. Good for pillar, wall, or fence.

'Casino', 3.5 m (12 ft). A vigorous climber; hybrid-tea-type flowers, deep yellow when young, but softening with age. Appreciates the shelter of a wall or pillar.

'Compassion', 2.4 m (8 ft). A vigorous grower; lovely hybrid-tea-type apricot-pink flowers with a considerable fragrance.

'Danse du Feu', 2.4 m (8 ft). A fairly vigorous climber; somewhat globular orange-scarlet flowers, set off nicely by dark-green foliage. Does well on a north wall, where it holds its spectacular colour better.

'Dortmund', 2.4 to 3 m (8 to 10 ft). A Kordes-type climber of vigorous growth; freely produced, large, single, crimson flowers with a white centre. Must be dead-headed for recurrent bloom, otherwise a large crop of hips supervenes. If it is pruned it makes a good shrub.

'Dreaming Spires'. A vigorous upright climber; impressive, bright golden yellow flowers and heavy, dark-green, leathery foliage. Has a distinct fragrance.

'Dublin Bay'. A climber of medium growth, 2 m (6 ft); very freely produced, double, brilliant deep-red flowers.

'Galway Bay', 2.4 to 3 m (8 to 10 ft). A vigorous climber; large, semi-double, salmon-pink flowers produced in abundance over a long period.

'Golden Showers', 2 to 3 m (6 to 10 ft). A variety of medium growth with almost thornless stems; freely produced, deep-gold flowers which pale to cream. Blooms with great consistency if regularly dead-headed. Successful as a shrub or a hedge, it is easily kept to its allotted space and so is particularly suitable for small gardens.

'Handel', 2.4 to 3 m (8 to 10 ft). A vigorous and distinctive rose; its shapely buds open cream, flushed and heavily edged with deep pink, and are freely produced. The young growths break freely from base, so with pruning it makes an excellent shrub.

'Joseph's Coat'. An all-rounder useful as a pillar rose or on a wall, where it will reach 3 m (10 ft) when trained; large trusses of semi-double, bright yellow flowers flushed with orange and cherry red. Very productive, especially in autumn. Can be grown as a shrub or, if heavily pruned, as a tall bedder.

'Mermaid', 7.6 m (25 ft). An outsider in this group, but included because of its long flowering period; delicately scented, beautiful single, pale sulphur-yellow flowers. Not a rose for cold districts, it is best suited to warm walls or close-boarded fences.

'Mme Alfred Carrière', 6.1 m (20 ft). A vigorous climber, almost a century old but included in this section

Three rose climbers: the two red varieties are (left) 'Dortmund' and (right) 'Raymond Chenault', both Kordes-types; the white in the foreground is 'Bobbie James'.

because it flowers recurrently; freely produced, small white flowers suffused with pale bluish pink. Popular owing to its ability to thrive on walls with northern and eastern aspects; useful also on a pergola or up and over an old tree.

'New Dawn', 2.1 m (7 ft). Although essentially a rambler it has been much used in breeding of recurrent climbers; medium-sized, fragrant, pale silvery pink flowers. Ideal for covering fences, or can be pruned to form a spreading shrub.

'Parade', 3 to 3.5 m (10 to 12 ft). A vigorous climber, also good for pillars; large, deep carmine-rose flowers, very freely produced and scented, but tending to droop slightly. It is especially

useful for walls of north or east aspect.

'Parkdirektor Riggers', 3.5 m (12 ft). A vigorous Kordes climber, suitable also for tall pillars; large clusters of semi-double, deep-crimson flowers, well set off by the glossy, dark-green foliage. Must be dead-headed for recurrent bloom.

'Pink Perpétué', 1.8 to 2.4 m (6 to 8 ft). A vigorous grower but restrained in height; double, clear, bright-pink flowers, carmine on the reverse side, giving a two-toned effect. Free flowering with attractive foliage, and ideal for pillars or fences.

'Rosy Mantle', 2.4 m (8 ft). A useful climber for fences, pillars, or walls; fragrant, double, light-pink flowers.

'Royal Gold', 2.4 m (8 ft). A fairly

vigorous grower; double, deep golden yellow hybrid-tea-type flowers. A fine variety, but it will not prosper on sites exposed to cold winds from the north or east.

'Schoolgirl', 2.4 to 3 m (8 to 10 ft). A vigorous climber; fragrant blooms in bright apricot-orange shades. Apt to become leggy at base.

'Swan Lake', 2.1 to 2.4 m (7 to 8 ft). A strong-growing rose with abundant foliage; well-formed, large, silvery white flowers tinged pink in centre. Resistant to wet weather. May need protection against black spot.

'White Cockade', 1.8 m (6 ft). A variety of restricted growth; shapely, double, white flowers. Useful for a low wall, fence, or pillar, or as a shrub.

'Zéphirine Drouhin': *see* Bourbon roses (p. 47), to which it belongs. It is included here because it is a recurrent flowering climber.

Tall growers

The vigorous ramblers and climbers listed below include several of the older varieties. Although all these varieties flower only once in the season, they are useful for covering tall structures such as arches, pergolas, and high walls, or for concealing an ugly shed.

'Albéric Barbier', 7.6 m (25 ft). A very vigorous rambler with almost evergreen foliage; pure yellow buds open to large double blooms of creamy white with some fragrance. Excellent for walls or for scrambling into an old tree. Flowers profusely.

'Albertine', 4.6 m (15 ft). A very vigorous, woody rambler; warm coppery pink buds open to strongly scented, salmon-pink flowers. Flowers early, and is abundant in June. A very popular variety, which should have some of the old flowering wood removed to encourage young vigorous growth. Excellent for walls or fences. Resists bad weather, but is inclined to mildew.

'Chaplin's Pink Climber'. A very vigorous grower, 3 m (10 ft) high, often used for covering fences; large, semi-double, bright pink flowers, perhaps a bit garish but certainly popular.

'City of York', 3.5 m (12 ft). A

'Aloha', a variety popular as a pillar rose.

rambler with considerable vigour; large, freely produced, fragrant creamy white flowers and luxuriant foliage.

'Climbing Cécile Brunner', 6.1 m (20 ft). A vigorous climber for a wall or fence; very free flowering, small, blush-pink blooms deepening towards the centre. Greatly admired by those who appreciate the delicate, hybrid-tea-like form of the flowers. Main display in June, but a few blooms later.

'Constance Spry', 2.4 m (8 ft). A very vigorous shrub rose which can be trained to pillars or walls, as it thrives with some support; large, well-formed, deep glowing pink flowers, paler towards the outside. Strongly scented, it has become very popular because of its sumptuous, old-world appearance.

'Crimson Shower', 2.4 m (8 ft). A vigorous rambler, which owes part of its popularity to the fact that it flowers late, when most non-recurrent varieties have finished; abundant, small, rosette-shaped, crimson flowers which last for a considerable period. Good for training on a bank or fence, or as a weeping standard. Prune old flowering growths away once flowering ends.

'Easlea's Golden Rambler', 3.7 m (12 ft). A vigorous rambler which is really a climber, and is thus suitable for pergola or pillar; strongly scented, large, semi-double, creamy yellow flowers of hybrid tea type. Flowers freely in June. Should be pruned back to young growths after flowering ceases.

'Félicité et Perpétué', 6 m (20 ft). A vigorous and extremely hardy rambler, often found on old walls facing north; creamy white, button-like flowers produced in masses. One of the most charming varieties, with a long season of flowering around mid-July.

'Francis E. Lester', 4.6 m (15 ft). A vigorous rambler; large clusters of strongly scented, small, single, creamy white flowers with a flush of pink becoming white. A fine specimen can be seen on the office wall of the RHS at Wisley. It has a crop of small oranged-red hips from October onwards. Lovely for growing on a small tree, or it will form a large bush.

'François Juranville', 7.6 m (25 ft). A vigorous rambler; strongly scented, salmon-pink flowers with somewhat quilled petals. An old favourite which will cover a large area on a pergola, or scramble into an old tree.

'Lawrence Johnston', up to 6 m (20 ft). A vigorous climber; spectacular, strongly scented, semi-double, bright-yellow flowers. Main display in June, with intermittent blooms later. Ideal for a pergola, as can be seen at the RNRS gardens at St Albans; can also be grown as a shrub if strong growths are shortened.

'Leverkusen', up to 3 m (10 ft). A Kordes climber of moderate vigour; scented, semi-double, creamy yellow flowers blend well with other varieties, and are freely produced. Main flowering period in June; a few recurrent blooms also occur.

'Maigold', 2.4 to 3.5 m (8 to 12 ft). A very vigorous, extremely thorny variety, which will attain maximum height on a wall; large, scented, semi-double, bronze-yellow blooms with yellow stamens. Flowers early in the season. Can also be grown as a large, open shrub, especially useful for planting against fences.

'Mme Grégoire Staechelin', up to 4.6 m (15 ft). A vigorous climber on a wall, where it is especially effective if grown against grey stone or white-painted bricks; sumptuous, large, scented, clear-pink blooms, with deeper reverse. Flowers early in June. Well suited to north-facing walls.

'Paul's Lemon Pillar', 3.5 m (12 ft). A vigorous climber; large, strongly scented, creamy yellow flowers of

'Zéphirine Drouhin', a useful climbing Bourbon.

hybrid tea type, sometimes almost of exhibition standard. A good wall rose.

'Paul's Scarlet Climber', 3 m (10 ft). A climber of medium vigour but of a profusely flowering habit; semi-double, scarlet-red flowers in clusters.

'Sanders' White Rambler', 3.5 m (12 ft). A vigorous rambler; small, scented, semi-double, white flowers in freely produced clusters. Most fragrant

of the many varieties of *Rosa wichuraiana*, it is ideal as a weeping standard. Prune away old flowering growths when flowering has finished.

'The Garland', 4.6 m (15 ft). A very vigorous rambler, sometimes found in old gardens where it is valued for its scent; very abundant pale creamy salmon flowers, fading to creamy white. Can be pruned to form a loose, open shrub, grown on a wall, or trained up a small tree.

'Veilchenblau', 3.7 m (12 ft). A vigorous rambler, often called the 'blue' rose because of its distinctive purple-violet colour. It is apt to fade to lilac grey in hot sun, so it should be planted in shade against a wall. It is sweetly fragrant.

'Violette'. Up to 4.6 m (15 ft) if growing in good soil; freely flowering, slightly scented, maroon-purple flowers, which fade to maroon-grey unless the plant is grown against a shady .

'Albertine', a vigorous climber for walls.

pergola or wall. An almost thornless variety.

'Wedding Day', 7.6 m (25 ft). A rampant rambler which readily grows over old garden sheds, barns, hedges, or up into trees; flower clusters are pale creamy yellow on opening, turning white and becoming pink-spotted as they age – a feature approved by some but disliked by others. Most imposing if grown as a standard, when its vigour can be controlled through the stem and by pruning.

Note I have omitted 'Dorothy Perkins' from this section. Although much loved, and still a feature of many cottage gardens, it is far too susceptible to mildew to deserve recommendation.

Right 'Climbing Cécile Brunner', a China rose.
Below 'Paul's Scarlet Climber', popular garden rose since its introduction in 1916.

10 Perfume in Roses

FOR many people, one of the keenest pleasures of growing roses comes from their fragrance. Nothing gives me greater joy than the scent of the leaves of the sweet briar, which can be particularly strong on a warm summer evening, especially after a shower of rain. The scent of its hybrids, the Penzance briars, is also very pleasing, although not quite so rich in quality. *Rosa primula* is well known as the incense rose from the strongly aromatic perfume not only of its leaves but of its wood. *R. setipoda* is also worth growing for the scent of its leaves, and it has passed this quality on to the hybrid *R. × wintoniensis*. Noteworthy also for their scent are the moss roses, and the flower stalks of some of the old garden roses, especially when crushed lightly in the hand.

Most appealing generally, however, is the perfume of the flowers themselves, a quality looked for first by many people. Having had a large public rose garden under my care for several years, this fact became very obvious to me. On entering the garden many visitors stopped to smell the rose blooms before making any attempt to take in the visual effect of the flowers, and generally moved on quickly to another variety in search of an even finer fragrance. It is often asserted that modern roses do not have the scent of the older varieties. In fact, many modern roses, particularly hybrid teas, are superbly fragrant, whereas some older roses have little, if any scent. Furthermore, some modern floribunda roses now have a fragrance that is even

sweeter than that of many hybrid teas.

Fragrance in roses is a very elusive quality, particularly when one tries to describe it. It depends to a certain extent on individual appreciation, which can and does differ considerably. Sensitivity to scents varies greatly amongst individuals. Tobacco smokers and sufferers from nasal catarrh are generally considered to be handicapped in their

ability to enjoy scent.

Blindness concentrates sensitivity on the other faculties, and blind people often have an enhanced sense of smell. For this reason they are sometimes asked to judge roses for fragrance. Some blind people have developed this talent to such an extent that they can instantly recognise individual varieties.

Climatic conditions, temperature,

and general humidity cause variations in the fragrance of flowers, while individual varieties diffuse their scent at different stages in the life of the flower – some early, others when fully open.

I have always found that scent is elusive when the temperature is low. Despite this, I think morning is the best time for rose scents, especially after a damp night when the sun has not yet raised the temperature but has dried the flowers. Perhaps the most pleasurable fragrance is that known as damask. This has long been associated with some of the old garden roses but is also to be found in several more modern varieties.

Most rosarians, while admitting the importance of fragrance, lay greater stress on form and colour when assessing a variety. The late Harry Wheatcroft, one of the world's most renowned rosarians, put it most succinctly when he insisted that 'the eye comes before the nose'. Nevertheless, fragrance undoubtedly plays a large part in the average rose grower's choice of varieties. The following are brief selections of fragrant roses of different types; those marked with an asterisk are the most strongly (although not necessarily the most attractively) scented.

Above left *Rosa setipoda*, a native of central China, was introduced into Europe some 70 years ago. Although rarely seen as a garden rose, it is well worth cultivating for its distinctive, fragrant foliage. **Right** 'Troika', a vigorous, upright hybrid tea with delightfully scented flowers.

Hybrid Tea Roses
'Adolph Horstmann'
★ 'Alec's Red'
'Alpine Sunset'
'Blessings'
★ 'Blue Moon'
'Champion'
'Dekorat'
'Diorama'
'Elizabeth Harkness'
'Ena Harkness'
'Ernest H. Morse'
★ 'Fragrant Cloud'
'Helen Traubel'
★ 'Josephine Bruce'

'Just Joey'
★ 'Lady Sylvia'
★ 'Mala Rubinstein'
'Mischief'
★ 'Mullard Jubilee'
'My Choice'
★ 'Northern Lights'
★ 'Ophelia'
★ 'Papa Meilland'
'Precious Platinum'
★ 'Prima Ballerina'
'Super Star'
'Susan Hampshire'
★ 'Sutter's Gold'
'Troika'

'Typhoon'
'Typhoo Tea'
★ 'Wendy Cussons'
'Whisky Mac'

Floribunda Roses
'Apricot Nectar'
★ 'Arthur Bell'
'Burma Star'
'Courvoisier'
'Dearest'
★ 'Elizabeth of Glamis'
★ 'Escapade'
★ 'Harry Edland'
'Iceberg'

'Isis'
'Korresia'
'Lilac Charm'
★ 'Margaret Merril'
'Matangi'
'Michelle'
'Moon Maiden'
★ 'Orange Sensation'
'Orange Silk'
'Pernille Poulsen'
★ 'Pineapple Poll'
'Rob Roy'
'Sea Pearl'
★ 'Sugar Sweet'
'Sunsilk'

Left 'Mullard Jubilee', a scented hybrid tea.

Scented Foliage

Rosa eglanteria, the sweet briar, is a native of Britain and Europe; its dense, prickly stems are frequently found in hedges, producing a spicy fragrance that emanates from glands on the underside of the leaves. It is especially noticeable in wet weather or on a warm summer evening. The single flowers in shades of pink are also scented and are followed by bright red hips. Sometimes it is recommended as a hedge in smaller gardens, but a single plant placed discreetly in the background will be sufficient to provide its perfume without disclosing the inelegance of the mature plant, especially as it is susceptible to black spot.

The hybrids usually known as the Penzance briars (they were sent out by Lord Penzance in 1894 and 1895) have become more popular than *R. eglanteria* because they are more robust in growth and more colourful in flower – although the scent of their foliage is usually less striking. The following are typical examples.

'Amy Robsart', up to 3 m (10 ft). Deep, clear-pink, semi-double flowers, followed by attractive scarlet hips.

'Anne of Geierstein'. Dark-crimson, single flowers succeeded by good hips. Medium-strong scent.

'Lady Penzance', 2 m (6 ft). Not as vigorous as other varieties, but has most attractive single, coppery salmon-pink flowers. Must be watched for black spot on its scented foliage.

'Lord Penzance'. Much like Lady Penzance in vigour; the single flowers are soft, rosy yellow, paler than those of Lady Penzance and less attractive. Foliage quite strongly scented.

'Meg Merrilees', 3 m (10 ft). Semi-double, crimson flowers are produced freely. One of the best of the hybrids, with both flowers and leaves nicely scented, and followed by bright-red hips. Makes a tall hedge, but somewhat liable to black spot.

Rosa glutinosa. An uncommon dwarf, which in fact I have never seen planted as an ornamental shrub. It has pine-scented foliage.

R. primula, 2.1 m (7 ft) and more. Produces its attractive creamy yellow, single flowers generally in May. The slight fragrance of the flowers is overshadowed by the strong scent, reminis-

cent of incense, that emanates from both the brown wood and the decorative ferny leaves of this fine shrub. This scent is readily carried on the slightest puff of wind, and one plant strategically placed near the garden door will provide much pleasure.

R. setipoda, up to 3 m (10 ft). A fine shrub worth growing where there is room for its handsome foliage, which is glandular underneath and scented as a sweet briar. The strength of the fragrance is greatly increased if the leaves are crushed in the hand. The

Above 'Harkuly' ('Margaret Merril'), one of the most fragrant floribundas. Below *Rosa eglanteria* (sweet briar), with spicy scented leaves.

beautifully formed pink flowers are followed by orange-red hips.

R. × wintoniensis. A hybrid more akin to *R. setipoda* than to its female parent, *R. moyesii*. The clusters of deep rose-pink flowers are followed by bristly orange-red hips. The scent of its foliage is similar in quality and strength to that of the sweet briar.

11 Designing a Rose Garden

THE design of a rose garden should be based as far as possible on personal preferences, but in a small garden it has also to be determined by the amount of available ground. Grass is a good background for roses of any type, but a garden which consists of many small beds cut out of a lawn tends to look fussy. Moreover it is difficult to maintain, for it complicates mowing and a great deal of edging work is necessary to keep a neat appearance. I much prefer an island bed, fine examples of which are those used for herbaceous plants at Bressingham Hall in Norfolk and at the Royal Horticultural Society's gardens at Wisley, and for roses in the display garden of the RNRS at St Albans. The RNRS island bed has been created with easy curves so that mowing does not cause any problems. The planting of compact cluster-flowered roses in groups has been given the added dimension of height by a few weeping standards, and plants such as *Juniperus* 'Blue Star' provide an additional effect with their interesting foliage. Around the sides, an informal border of shrub roses has been planted, mainly to show varieties which can be accommodated in a small garden. In a private garden this idea could be adapted to one's personal preference by the planting, for instance, of groups of hybrid teas or floribunda roses.

Another small garden at St Albans is a sort of negative image of the one mentioned above. It consists of an almost circular lawn with informal groups of roses, arranged according to colour, planted in groups around the perimeter. A stone bird bath placed in the middle of the lawn provides a focal point. In small town gardens grass can be impractical, and paving or bricks may be more sensible. Creeping plants, in particular the various thymes, can be planted near the edges to soften the appearance. Without doubt real stone looks best, but stone substitutes will weather in time and become acceptable.

All rose gardens should have a space, either on the lawn or on paving, large enough to take two or three comfortable garden chairs. It is always a great pleasure merely to sit down among them and enjoy their colour, form, and fragrance with one's friends.

Generally, when taking on a new garden, every effort will be made to get something to grow and flower as quickly as possible. Roses can be in flower in four months, certainly not at their best, but good enough to give some pleasure.

Lovers of hybrid teas will probably prefer a fairly formal plan for their roses. The best design is probably a simple one, with rectangular beds which will hold at least three rows of plants. This permits a bold display while allowing access to the plants. The beds can be designed for long term use (*see* Chapter 3) by leaving enough grass between them to accommodate replacement beds after 12 or 15 years. Such a formal garden will be rather flat, but it can be relieved by the introduction of a few standards. Alternatively, tripods or similar structures can be covered with pillar roses. To make maintenance easy, these should be placed in the bed rather than isolated on the lawn, unless you want to use them as a background. The traditional pergolas and arches are not only expensive to build but require more attention than most amateur gardeners can afford. Floribunda roses can be fitted into informal surroundings more readily than the hybrid tea, with its large formal flowers.

The older shrub roses are of course completely at home in informal surroundings, where their more subtle colourings do not suffer in comparison with the strong orange-reds of many of the modern roses. Odd as it may seem, the design of an informal rose garden in some respects requires more careful planning than a formal one. The very fact that the roses will not be planted in more or less straight rows or in geometric patterns means that you must give thought to the spaces between the plants and to the often considerable sizes that mature shrub roses attain. For instance, one of the finest and most popular varieties, 'Nevada', is well able to reach a height and width of 2 m (6 ft) within five years. The question of pruning also needs to be taken into account. Admittedly pruning is much less of a problem in an informal garden – but when it becomes necessary, it is much easier and pleasanter to do if you can tackle the plant without getting entangled in the foliage and thorns of its neighbours.

Formal rose beds. Visual interest can be increased by careful selection of differently coloured varieties.

12 Pruning

A GREAT deal has been written about the pruning of roses, much of it sensible, but some is liable to confuse the newcomer to rose growing. Pruning is of course of considerable interest to rosarians, and is a subject that causes much discussion and even controversy among keen rose growers. The beginner, however, would be justified in posing the question 'why prune?', and indeed in querying whether it is really necessary.

Roses can sometimes be seen flowering away in somewhat neglected gardens where little attention has been given to pruning. This is permissible for a season, but closer inspection over a longer period will reveal a considerable amount of deterioration in the plants. Long, untidy, straggling growths will predominate, with few flowers and those few of poor quality. Usually the bush becomes cluttered with dead and diseased growth, and sometimes it will be dominated by suckers from the rootstock, presenting a derelict appearance quite unacceptable to anyone who loves gardens. Contrast this with the garden where the roses have been pruned intelligently so as to encourage strong healthy growth by removing old and worn wood. Shaping the bush so that it fits into its surroundings is also particularly important in small gardens. From this it should be clear that in order to produce good results pruning is necessary.

Roses vary widely in habit, from the tiny miniatures, which can be invaluable in very small gardens and window boxes, to the mighty scramblers which are acceptable only in large gardens. Variation in habit calls for variation in treatment, but this need not be confusing if the basic principles are understood. This essentially means the removal of any dead or diseased growths, as well as those which have become old, weak, or unproductive. It is extremely important that light and air reach the centre of the plant, so any cross growths which impede this should be removed at source. Weak growths or those damaged in any way are unlikely to produce good flowers, so these too are better removed.

Readers of this book will probably be mainly concerned with hybrid tea and floribunda roses, which are more easily accommodated in small gardens and also in general flower over a longer period.

These types of rose produce their flowers on growth of the current year, as do climbers. Ramblers, species roses (the wild roses), many shrub roses, and old garden roses generally flower on growths made in the previous year. It is important therefore to know which group you are dealing with, otherwise you may prune away the flowering growths.

When to prune

When pruning should be done has always been fiercely debated, but it should really depend, predominantly, on climate and conditions. Those who are fortunate enough to live in warm areas, especially if close to the sea and perhaps under the influence of the Gulf Stream, can prune early, in about November. In more austere environments, such as exposed gardens on the eastern coast of England, those in the north, and those at high altitudes, it is usual to shorten back long growths at this time to prevent 'wind rock', but to leave the main pruning to March or April. The farther north and the more exposed the garden is, the later should pruning be carried out. Pruning during periods of severe frost should be avoided if possible, as damage may occur. Planning to prune at a certain time can be unsatisfactory; weather conditions should be taken into account, and these obviously can vary from year to year.

How to prune

Beginners pruning hybrid tea roses that are maiden trees (that is, first-year plants), should prune them fairly severely, cutting the growths back to two or three eyes from the base so that the uppermost eye faces outwards. (An 'eye' is an undeveloped growth bud that appears in the axil of a leaf – that is the angle between the stem and the leaf stalk.) Good plants will generally have three or four strong growths, which will be enough to make a well-balanced bush. When a plant is estab-

Intelligent pruning allows the gardener to shape his roses, encourages their growth, and helps to keep them healthy.

Pruning a newly planted rose. Always cut back to outward-facing buds or eyes.

Light pruning of bush roses every year encourages development of many blooms.

Hard pruning encourages fewer but finer blooms, important with hybrid teas.

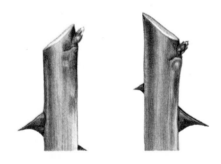

Pruning cuts: correct (left) and incorrect. The cut should slope down away from the bud, which should be outward facing.

lished after the initial year's growth, moderate pruning to five or six eyes will produce the best shape for the garden, but care must be taken to remove completely all small, twiggy growths. Always aim for an open, cup-shaped formation, cutting away any growths which tend to clutter up the centre. All soft, unripened growths should be cut out completely, especially in northern and exposed gardens. In these gardens after a severe winter, hard pruning may be necessary, as it is only by doing so that sound wood near the base of the plant will be left. Growths affected by frost will have brown pith, so cutting back until white pith is found is necessary.

Some varieties produce basal growths, and these should be encouraged by cutting out older growths to give the new growths room. Pruning back one growth each year almost

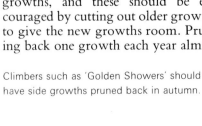

Climbers such as 'Golden Showers' should have side growths pruned back in autumn.

to ground level often induces these basal growths to form, thus ensuring young replacement wood and preventing leggy trees from developing.

Pruning cuts should be sloping, the highest point being about 6 mm ($\frac{1}{4}$ in) above the eye with the lowest point behind, but not touching, the eye. A sharp pair of secateurs should be used to make a clean cut.

Pruning floribunda roses is carried out as for hybrid teas in the first year. Afterwards lighter pruning is sufficient, as masses of flowers are expected from this type. Many floribundas break very freely from near the base of the plant, a trend readily encouraged by removal of older growths when the opportunity arises, and shortening young growths by a third.

Miniature roses sometimes require slightly different treatment. Normal growths can be pruned back to three or four eyes, cutting out weak growths. Some varieties are apt to produce very strong growths which spoil the symmetry of the plant. These should be removed entirely or cut back severely to maintain the compact habit which is desirable in this type of rose.

Standard roses (or tree roses, as they are sometimes known) are popular with many amateurs, and they can be useful in small gardens for adding height to a bed. Generally they have been derived from hybrid tea or floribunda roses, so the treatment advocated for bush roses can be applied. However, I prefer to prune these roses severely because they derive their nourishment through one long stem, which sometimes restricts vigour. If they are only lightly pruned and a large head develops they are likely to be damaged by wind, especially in open and exposed gardens. I would generally prune to three or four eyes in order to prevent this.

Weeping standards seem to have lost favour to a certain extent, but when they are grown the best results are obtained from those which produce pendulous growth. The *R. wichuraiana* varieties such as 'Crimson Shower' are ideal for this purpose. Pruning away the old flowering growths after they have flowered is all that is required if sufficient young growths have been produced. If they have not, it is advisable to retain some of the older growths, reducing side growths to about one or two eyes.

Some of our most attractive climbing roses are sports from bush hybrid teas; like their parents they produce flowers on growths of the current year. Some are very vigorous and inclined to produce growth at the expense of flowers if they are subjected to much pruning. If these strong growths are trained horizontally on a wall or fence, lateral flowering growths are induced which will produce flowers. These can be shortened back to a couple of eyes in the spring. Vigorous young growths are also produced from the base by some varieties, and if possible these should be retained, older growth being cut away in order to accommodate them. Unripe tip growths or those

Vigorous shrub roses like 'Marguerite Hilling' should have older woody stems pruned.

which encroach beyond their allotted space should also be removed.

Rose species and their hybrids seldom require pruning except to keep them to their allotted space. Dead growths, of course, are valueless and should be removed, as should the occasional old growth, especially if young growths near the base require room.

Ramblers bred from *R. wichuraiana*, such as 'Crimson Shower', should be pruned as soon as flowering is over by removal of the old flowering growths. September is generally the time for this. Hybrids such as the favourites 'Albertine' and 'Alberic Barbier' do not produce young basal growths in this manner and have to have a growth or two cut back before they will do so. Likewise, growths higher up have to be cut back to where young growths have started. Young growths

should of course be retained and laterals (side shoots) reduced to two or three eyes in spring.

Repeat-flowering climbers generally flower on lateral growths, which should be pruned back to a few eyes in autumn. Young growths should be trained horizontally or spiralled around poles or tripods to produce flowering laterals and young basal growth. Old flower heads should be removed, unless hips are wanted, in order to extend the season of flowering.

For those with larger gardens, shrub roses have long been popular. Few of these require pruning the first season after planting. Most shrub roses flower on the previous season's growth, so this can be encouraged by removing shoots that have flowered back to a strong young growth. Any dead or exhausted growths can be cut back to the base of the plant.

Very vigorous shrubs benefit from the removal of at least some old woody stems and any weak or worn-out growths. Very strong growths may be reduced by a third in order to lessen wind rock and to improve shape.

Several types of roses are useful as informal hedges. Rugosa roses, sweet briar, Scotch roses, and *Rosa gallica officinalis* ('Versicolor') in particular are suitable. These can be trimmed with shears during the winter months, as many formal hedges are. Many other shrub roses and vigorous floribundas may also be used in hedges, but they are better pruned by secateurs.

13 Propagation

MANY amateur gardeners derive great satisfaction from propagating their own roses. There are four basic methods of doing this: by budding, cuttings, layering, and seeds.

Budding

The majority of roses grown in the United Kingdom by commercial growers are propagated by the method known as budding, a technique in which a dormant bud of the required variety is inserted under the bark of a rootstock. This system has several advantages; in particular, it makes for rapid and uniform growth of a plant in full possession of vigour from the rootstock. It is particularly valuable in the case of new or scarce varieties, since only one bud is required to produce a plant; in consequence, multiplication can be quite rapid, especially in the hands of an experienced propagator. A good plant can be expected to provide as many as 50 buds in one season, and some of the more robust varieties have been known to produce many more.

I have always been fascinated when visiting rose nurseries in July and August to see the skill and speed with which specialist budders cut out the buds and insert them in the T-shaped cut made in the rootstock. An assistant closes the cut bark around the bud with a plastic or rubber tie stretched over the bud and fixed with a wire staple. These ties eventually disinte-

grate as the stock swells. Within a few weeks, close examination will ascertain whether or not the bud has 'taken'. If successful, the stalk 'handle' attached to the bud drops off; but if the handle and bud remain brown and shrivelled, it indicates that the union has failed. In this case another bud can be inserted in a new cut made in the opposite side of the rootstock.

Budding is a simple surgical operation which should be performed with reasonable speed, although it takes time to acquire the manipulative skill of the professional. Special budding knives are available in which the handle tapers off so that it can be used to lift the bark of the stock. Remember always to keep the blade of the knife clean (it may carry disease organisms) and very sharp.

In nurseries nowadays dwarf stocks are invariably planted, by machine, about 20 cm (8 in) apart, with 1 m (3 ft) between the rows. These distances allow mechanical cultivation, spraying, and lifting to be carried out, but they are modified by some growers to suit their particular methods or circumstances. Amateurs and small growers who operate on a less ambitious scale generally plant by hand, and rows 600 mm (2 ft) apart will be found quite satisfactory. Plant the stocks so that they lean at a slight angle, which makes budding easier, and place the roots just below ground level. On completion of planting, draw some soil up by hoe to cover the stem. This helps to prevent the bark becoming hard and difficult to open for bud insertion. Plant in well-prepared soil

from December onwards, ending in March in southern England, but extending into April in colder areas.

Stocks are grown mainly by continental specialists, although in recent years interest in stock production has increased in England. Modern stocks, grown from seed, have the great advantage of a good root system, which transplants happily and is less likely to be affected by virus diseases. These stocks are graded after a season's growth and are generally available in stem thicknesses of from 3 to 5 mm, 4 to 6 mm, 5 to 8 mm, and 8 to 12 mm. Nurserymen generally plant the 5 to 8 mm ($\frac{3}{16}$ to $\frac{5}{16}$ in) size, which grow rapidly in late summer, when rootstocks will reach 12 mm ($\frac{1}{2}$ in) in diameter. Those who wish to bud early, especially if buds are available from roses grown under glass, will find the larger sizes easier to work with. Northern growers almost invariably use the larger rootstocks. This is because their climate enforces late planting and causes slower growth.

In general, budding is carried out during the months of July and August, when the stock is in active growth and the bark lifts easily. Soil should be drawn away from the rootstock with a hoe or trowel as far down as the roots. Clean the stem with a duster or piece of cloth to prevent soil getting into the T-cut. If the stock has been planted on the slant, push its top growth further over to one side, placing a foot on it to keep it out of the way. Make the cross cut of the T about 25 mm (1 in) above the roots, and deep enough to penetrate the soft bark and free it without

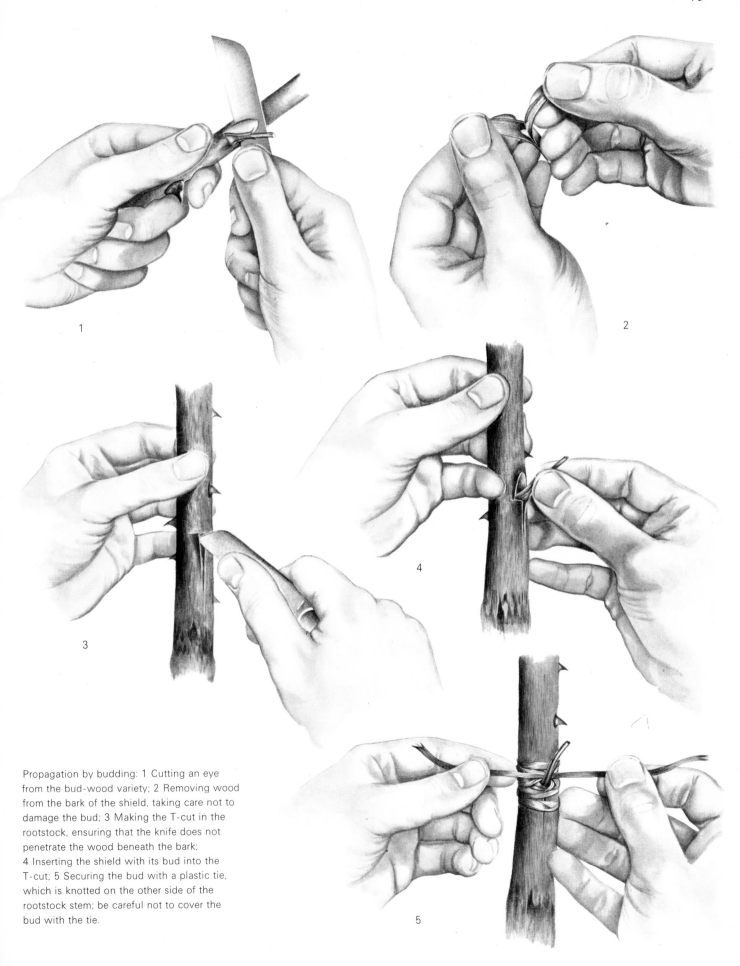

Propagation by budding: 1 Cutting an eye from the bud-wood variety; 2 Removing wood from the bark of the shield, taking care not to damage the bud; 3 Making the T-cut in the rootstock, ensuring that the knife does not penetrate the wood beneath the bark; 4 Inserting the shield with its bud into the T-cut; 5 Securing the bud with a plastic tie, which is knotted on the other side of the rootstock stem; be careful not to cover the bud with the tie.

Plant stem cuttings about 150 mm (6 in) apart.

Air layering with a flexible-stemmed variety.

injuring the wood beneath. Complete the T by cutting the bark downwards towards the roots from the middle of the cross cut. Now reverse the knife, using the end of the handle to lift the bark away in two flaps. If growth is active the bark should lift cleanly, but it may be resistant if the weather has been dry. In such cases, watering a few days previously should have ensured the correct condition.

Bud-wood of the required cultivar should be selected from a healthy plant on which some of the flowers have just faded. The correct stage of maturity can be gauged by testing the thorns, which should snap off easily. The best buds are to be found around the middle of the stem; those at the base are too recessed, while those just under the flowers are usually too far advanced to be used. Cut off a growth 200–300 mm (8–12 in) in length containing three or four buds; remove all thorns and leaves, leaving 12 mm ($\frac{1}{2}$ in) of stalk for use as a handle. Label it with the name of the variety (this is especially important if you are budding more than one variety), and place it in a container of water until required. An eye should now be cut from the bud stick, starting 12 mm ($\frac{1}{2}$ in) above the bud and drawing the knife blade shallowly under it, so as to cut as little wood as possible, and then bringing the knife out at a similar distance on the other side of the bud. Because of the convex shape of the growth you will find that a little wood adheres behind the bud; this should be removed unless

it is extremely thin. The secret of success lies here, as the growing tissue (cambium layer) beneath the bud and bark must come into direct contact with the cambium layer of the root-stock. Take great care not to damage the bud when removing the wood behind the eye.

You now should have a 'shield' of bark containing the bud. Holding it by the handle, push the bud down into the T-cut as far as it will go under the flaps. Any surplus bark above the cross cut should be removed. Stretch a plastic tie over the bud, and bring the wire staple around behind the stock and attach it to the other end of the tie. Some amateurs prefer to use raffia, instead of the plastic tie. This should be cut into lengths of about 450 mm (18 in) and kept moist. Make sure that you do not cover the eye.

When budding has been completed, the soil which was removed earlier can be drawn back over the roots of the stock. Union between bud and stock takes place quickly, and in three weeks time, if raffia has been used, the ties will have become too tight and a couple of strands will have to be cut carefully in order to ease it and prevent swelling.

In January or February, heading back should be carried out. This involves removing that part of the root-stock above the inserted bud, leaving a stump about 25 mm (1 in) long. (Incidentally, if you have bought new plants from a rose nurseryman you may find that he has neglected to remove the dead stump above the union of bud and rootstock.) Occasionally a few buds start into growth soon after budding and these should be cut back to two basal buds. Most buds, however, will remain dormant until the plant has been headed back.

In order to prevent the wind blowing out the young growth from its

stock, it is worth supporting each plant with a 600 mm (2 ft) cane tied to the stock. 'Blowing out' takes place more readily with some stocks than others. *R. multiflora,* in particular, has gained some notoriety in this respect, and those with exposed gardens would be well advised to avoid this stock unless they are prepared to put up with considerable losses. Many nurserymen who cannot undertake staking lessen the risk by pinching back the first growth to 100 mm (4 in), which causes a delay of at least a fortnight in flowering. Rose exhibitors who favour flowers from 'maidens', as those new plants are called, can manipulate flowering dates in some degree by this

method. Pinching back also encourages bushiness.

Budding roses in quantity is quite a strenuous activity and can be taxing for the amateur gardener. If you are interested in this method, you would be well advised to begin with budding half or full standards, which at least is easier on the back muscles. Half-standards are about 750 mm (2½ ft) high, standards about 1.1 m (3½ ft), and weeping standards about 1.5 m (5 ft).

The method employed is the same as described for bush plants. The fine old standards sometimes seen in well-established gardens are usually grown on very vigorous stems which were culled from hedges and woodland areas by itinerant workers and supplied to nurseries in the autumn. When planted up in rows they were budded when well rooted and making free growth. This source of supply has virtually disappeared and the workers have found more lucrative methods of

Below left and below Standard roses are normally propagated by inserting two or three buds into main stems that have reached the required height.

making a living. If you are lucky enough to find an available source of *Rosa canina* (dog rose), they should be budded on side stems which have grown to the correct height. Choose three or four of the best buds, rubbing out or removing any others. Insert the buds on the top side, as near as possible to the parent stem. Such standards are exceedingly hardy and long lived. I have had very good results from *R. canina* 'Pfander', a stock which produces uniform stems rapidly, is fairly easy to bud, and produces few thorns; although it readily produces suckers, these are easily recognized and can be quickly removed. 'Pfander' is also reputed to give longer life than standards on *R. rugosa*.

As standard stems are only one year old when transplanted for budding the following year, the buds can be inserted into the main stem at the required height. Commercial growers usually insert two buds, but amateurs can insert an extra bud to provide an evenly balanced head, staggering them on different sides of the stem.

The most generally used stock for standards is a selected form of *R. rugosa* which, when pruned back hard

the following spring, produces stems 1.5 to 2 m (5 to 6 ft) tall in the second year. Unfortunately some of these stems, which appear quite normal when budded, are infected with strawberry ringspot virus, so that growth from the buds is inhibited and unhealthy. Such stems should be removed and burned as soon as the disease is apparent, and the supplier informed.

Stocks

During the past decade much research has been carried out on rose stocks to help commercial growers to select the best for their purpose. Previously, the dog rose, *R. canina*, was most commonly used. At one time it was grown from cuttings and later from seed known as *R. canina* 'Wild'; the seedlings varied widely in quality and vigour and many produced suckers very freely – indeed, far too freely to satisfy the ultimate growers. Some cultivated forms, grown from seed and providing much more uniform growth and less inclination to send up suckers, have resulted in a decline in the use of the 'Wild' form; but an ideal replacement has not yet been found.

Most generally grown at the present time, largely because of its low production of suckers, is a variety of *R. dumetorum* known generally by commercial growers as 'Laxa'. Many growers raise roses under the protection of glass or polythene, in some cases to produce early blooms, but also to produce early buds. As 'Laxa' stock begins growth early, it is very suitable for early budding, producing strong growth which makes a high-quality plant, and it is easy to bud.

R. multiflora and its cultivar 'Inermis', which has few thorns, are also popular stocks which make rapid growth and large plants. When grown from seed they produce a good stock for floribundas, but they also suffer from some disadvantages. They do not grow successfully on alkaline soils and produce many surface roots, which are apt to suffer in dry weather and may make budding more difficult. They also break into growth early, so that growers in cold areas have found them unsuitable, and transplanting can be uncertain as the root system is apt to dry out. Some sweet briar, *R. eglanteria* (*R. rubiginosa*), is also grown, mainly for late budding, but because it is thorny in the extreme, and therefore unpleasant to handle, it is not a favourite with budders.

Varieties of *R. canina*, which at the present time are used in smaller numbers, include 'Brogs', with few thorns; 'Heinsohn's Rekord', with few thorns and easy to bud; 'Inermis', with hardly any thorns and easy to bud; 'Pfander' (already mentioned), with hardly any thorns and fairly easy to bud; 'Pollmers', with few thorns and fairly easy to bud; 'Schmid's Ideal', thorny but fairly easy to bud; and 'Superbe', with few thorns and easy to bud. Plants produced on these stocks differ in various ways, including resistance to disease, number of flowers and suckers produced, and in the size of the mature plant.

Cuttings

Except for some specialists whom I will mention later, nurserymen do not find it worth while to try to produce roses on their own roots. There are various reasons for this, but one is outstanding: in these days of grading, lack of uniformity in the crop is an insuperable obstacle to commercial success. Other reasons include the amount of plant material required, which is of course much greater; the time it takes to produce good saleable plants; the variation which occurs in varieties; and the development, especially among hybrid teas, of unsatisfactory rooting systems which do not transplant successfully.

However, all these difficulties can be overlooked by keen amateurs, who often prefer to have roses on their own roots because any suckers which arise will come not from a rootstock but will be of the variety which is being grown. Cuttings root best when the wood is well ripened in the autumn, generally during September and early October. Shoots should be about 230 mm (9 in) in length and should not be from old growth, which is unlikely to make the cell changes necessary to produce roots.

The cutting should be cut off squarely under a leaf node; roots can be encouraged to develop by dipping this end into a hormone rooting powder. Leaves can be removed, except for two or three at the top; the cuttings are then inserted up to these leaves, which should mean at least two thirds under the soil. Taking out a small trench in a sheltered border where the soil is not cold and wet is probably the best method, and rooting can be hastened by the addition of some sharp sand in the trench bottom. Place the cuttings 150 mm (6 in) apart, allowing 300 mm (1 ft) between rows. Fill in the trench, firming the soil well; give it a soaking with water if it is dry.

Many varieties grow readily from cuttings. Indeed, in many districts this has led to the popularity of particular varieties, cuttings having been passed on to friends and neighbours. Ramblers, in particular 'American Pillar', 'Albertine', 'Chaplin's Pink Climber', 'Dorothy Perkins' and 'Goldfinch', have benefited greatly from this form of propagation; indeed, they are frequently overplanted, leaving little if any space in gardens for more attractive varieties. Many of the more vigorous floribundas, which produce firm, hard, pencil-thick growths, root quite readily, as also do hybrid teas. The exceptions are those varieties that produce pithy growth, which makes it difficult to root the cuttings.

Shrub and climbing species are generally propagated commercially by budding, except for species such as *R. spinosissima*, *R. rugosa*, and *R. virginiana*, which sucker freely. Those grown from either cuttings or suckers are an advantage for the amateur, as only suckers of the parent will be produced, and eventually these will produce nice clumps or thickets. Some other shrub roses which can readily be propagated from ripened wood cuttings are the hybrid or Pemberton musks, hybrid China roses, and hybrid perpetuals.

Miniature roses have increased in popularity in recent years and are being produced commercially from cuttings. This is carried out under glass, using young wood and the modern method of mist propagation. Budded or grafted plants are apt to grow rather tall, and many rosarians believe that these delightful plants retain their true character if grown on their own roots. Some amateurs also use mist units for propagating miniature roses, particularly during summer months. Alternatively, young growths can be placed as cuttings in a sandy mixture in September and kept in a closed propagating frame, either in a greenhouse or a larger cold frame; when rooted, they are put in individual pots and kept under protection for the first winter.

Layering

If only a few plants are required, roses with long flexible stems can be increased by layering. Multiflora-type ramblers and those bred from *R. wichuraiana* root easily by this method; indeed 'Temple Bells', a cultivar closely related to that species, will, if grown as a ground-cover shrub, root naturally where it comes into contact with the soil. The stem can be cut halfway through or some bark removed some way back from the growing tip, and if it is pegged down into a sand-peat compost, rooting will soon take place, especially if the compost is kept moist. A year or so afterwards the new growth can be separated by cutting the section of stem between the new roots and the parent plant, and it can then be planted where required.

Seeds

Roses can be raised from seed, although this is by no means the best way of propagating plants of good quality. Some seedsmen offer seed of so-called 'Fairy' roses, *R. chinensis minima* or *R. multiflora nana*. If sown in a little heat under glass in spring, these will produce small pink flowers on a dwarf plant in three or four months. The experienced rosarian will not be particularly impressed by their quality, but there is undoubtedly a great deal of satisfaction gained by the inexperienced amateur in raising plants from seed.

Seeds obtainable from seedsmen, or from botanic gardens, will often produce plants reasonably true to type or with useful variations. Much depends on the species, where the seeds were collected, and whether they were isolated from other species.

This is, of course, Nature's method of increasing the rose population, but few of the plants for our gardens or parks are produced in this way. It would not be satisfactory to do so, because modern garden roses are so complex in parentage that they do not breed true.

For many years now the interest in the production of new rose varieties has been tremendous. Breeders annually raise hundreds of thousands of seedlings, bred from seed and pollen parents specially selected in the attempt to improve on the thousands of varieties already in existence. Few succeed. The rest fail for any or all of a number of reasons, such as bad growing habit, poor flowers, susceptibility to disease, and so on. It is a very chancy business. Nevertheless, in spite of lack of facilities, gifted amateurs occasionally produce varieties that the greatest professional breeders might envy. Indeed, one amateur, A. Norman of Surrey, raised 'Ena Harkness', a very famous hybrid tea, 'Frensham', an equally famous floribunda, 'Crimson Shower', a fine climber, and several other varieties.

Above left 'Scabrosa', a form of *R. rugosa*, can be raised from suckers (shoots that develop below ground level). **Left** Miniatures like 'Dresden Doll' are most easily propagated by cuttings raised under glass.

14 Pests and Diseases

Roses, like other plants, are liable to be attacked by pests and diseases. The new-comer to rose-growing soon comes to accept this unfortunate truth. He also learns that the damage that can be caused by insects and disease organisms can be lessened considerably if he inspects his plants regularly, learns to recognize danger signals early, and takes prompt action; and that only buds from healthy plants should be used for propagation.

Much research has been devoted to the problems of plant pests and diseases, and at least some of the results of that research can be used effectively by the amateur gardener. Two important general points should be made about various proprietary products available for controlling pests and diseases. First, these products have been carefully formulated to do a specific job, so always make a point of reading carefully the manufacturers' instructions for their use and following these instructions to the letter. Second, many of the chemicals used in such products are poisonous. Take great care to keep them out of the reach of young children and animals and, as a matter of routine, wear rubber gloves when using them.

Insecticides should be used in moderation. Over-use is not only a waste of money: it may be counter-productive by enabling pests to develop resistance to the poisons. In general, a spray in mid-May followed by another in mid-June will usually be an adequate preventive treatment. A 'clearing-up' application of spray in September may also be beneficial.

Pests

APHIDS The most common and most prolific of pests. Most gardeners are familiar with these tiny insects, which are found on roses under the flower buds, particularly on young soft growth. They are also called greenfly, although there are many species which may be amber, reddish, black, or grey as well as green. Natural predators such as ladybirds, sparrows, and tits – or a sharp squirt of water from a hose – will certainly dispose of some aphids but will not as a general rule control them completely.

Aphids reproduce rapidly, so it is wise to spray them with an insecticide twice within three days to ensure eradication. Early in the season a fine, mist-like spray of malathion is effective; in warm summer temperatures of 18°C (65°F) or more I find that nicotine is still one of the most effective cures. Alternatively derris, which is harmless to most animals, may be used. (But note that it is deadly to fish, so avoid using it if your garden contains an ornamental pond or running water.) A more recent preparation, formothion, is an effective systemic insecticide – that is, a poison that a plant is able to absorb without any harm to itself and that will attack a sap-sucking insect such as an aphid. Formothion can be watered into the soil around the plant and will be taken up by the plant's roots.

CAPSID BUGS The presence of these insects is indicated by the tattered and often contorted appearance of shoot tips. The adult insect, about 6 mm ($\frac{1}{4}$ in) in length, is metallic green in colour. It moves rapidly if disturbed, and is best dealt with by use of a systemic insecticide such as fenitrothion. Spray both plants and soil.

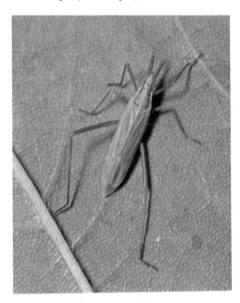

CATERPILLARS of various butterflies and moths feed on rose leaves and also attack buds on occasion. Generally shot-holed leaves are the most familiar sign, but leaf edges also suffer some damage. If only a few plants are affected, you can usually pick off the caterpillars by hand – but make sure to look on both sides of every leaf. If damage is more widespread, use a

Above Capsid bug. **Right** Seven-spot ladybirds eating aphids on a 'Frensham' (floribunda) bud.

systemic insecticide such as feni-trothion.

FROGHOPPER OR CUCKOO-SPIT INSECT
An insect easily identified by the frothy sap or spittle-like mass which gives the small yellow nymph protection. If only a few are present, you can kill them by squeezing them between your finger and thumb. Larger numbers will require the use of an insecticide sprayed with enough force to penetrate the protective spittle. Malathion is effective as an insecticide; a systemic insecticide will also aid control.

LEAF-ROLLING SAWFLY has become something of a menace in recent years, particularly in rose gardens that have sheltered corners or are overhung by trees – areas in which the fly likes to hover. The pest, the adult of which looks rather like a flying ant, causes rose leaves to roll or curl up. Once this has happened, it is too late to spray, and picking off by hand and burning becomes the only remedy. Preventive spraying in May and June, using either malathion or trichlorophon, should help to lessen the damage.

side of the leaves, which soon become an unhealthy blanched bronze in colour and later fall prematurely. A fine silky web is a sure pointer to the presence of this pest, which quickly builds up a resistance to some pesticides (as I have found with malathion). Systemic insecticides or liquid derris can be tried. Preventive measures include the clearing away of any weeds or rubbish around the plants.

LEAF-CUTTING BEES are similar in appearance to ordinary hive bees. The female cuts semi-circular portions neatly out of rose leaves, which she uses in the brood cells of her nest. The damage done, however, is not extensive enough to warrant destruction of the nests.

ROSE SLUG SAWFLY lays its eggs in May on the edges of young leaves. The resulting larvae, almost transparent, devour the internal tissues of the leaves until only a silvery skeleton is left. Spray both sides of the leaves with malathion or trichlorophon in May and June; a second spraying in July or August may also be necessary.

Gardeners generally find it is sensible also to take some positive preventive action against diseases. Coating both the upper and lower sides of the leaves with a fungicide will prevent disease spores from germinating. When in active growth, roses produce new leaves fairly rapidly, so fortnightly applications may be necessary. Weather conditions also have to be allowed for, and if there has been heavy rain it may be necessary to renew the protective cover. This is where the systemic fungicides now available are particularly useful, as they are absorbed into the plant tissues and provide internal protection.

Dusting may be easier than spraying, but it is generally less effective. Spraying, however, should not be done in hot sunshine; if possible choose a calm, dry evening. You will get better coverage if you use rainwater for mixing or diluting chemicals.

BLACK SPOT has been aptly termed 'clean-air disease': it rarely attacks roses in industrial areas. Indeed, the Clean Air Act, which has led to a vast improvement in atmospheric conditions all over urban Britain, is sometimes regarded with mixed feelings by rosarians contemplating the havoc caused by this disease.

Much has been written about black spot, which shows itself first as small spots with fringed edges. Appearing initially on the lower leaves, sometimes as early as May, it is generally

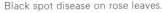

Black spot disease on rose leaves.

Leaves damaged by leaf-rolling sawfly.

THRIPS OR THUNDER FLIES These tiny, black-winged insects damage petal margins in very hot weather, and sometimes cause discoloration and distortion of young growth and buds. Damage is generally confined to roses with light-coloured flowers, particularly the 'Ophelia' group. Spray early in the season, applying derris, malathion, or nicotine, concentrating especially on the tips of young growths and buds.

RED-SPIDER MITES can be a serious pest in very hot, dry seasons on roses in warm, sheltered situations. The almost microscopic mites are difficult to detect; moreover, they live on the under-

Diseases

Growers are fortunate in that there are ways of controlling most disease organisms that infect roses. Good cultivation not only helps to produce handsome roses but is also the gardener's first line of defence against disease. As with insect pests, much can also be gained by a regular and close examination of plants for early symptoms of disease.

more noticeable from early August through to October, especially in periods of hot weather. In a severe attack, the disease spreads higher up the plant; the leaves turn yellow and drop prematurely, so that the whole plant becomes defoliated. This weakens the bush, and the effect of this may be noticeable the following season. Attacks vary in intensity from year to year and in different areas. The southwestern region of England seems to be particularly favourable to the disease.

Protection before infection is all important, and some growers spray the bushes and soil surface with a copper fungicide while the roses are dormant. After pruning, spraying with maneb has proved effective, and many gardeners have used the partially systemic benomyl with success; zineb and captan have also proved effective, as has a new preparation containing bupirimate and triforine.

POWDERY MILDEW is easily recognized by the white mould which resembles a sprinkling of flour on the leaves; when severe it becomes felt-like in appearance. Over-generous use of nitrogenous fertilizers, which produce young, soft growth, is a contributory factor, and dryness at the roots also encourages the spread of the disease. It is often particularly noticeable on climbers close to walls or fences where it is difficult for rain to reach. 'Dorothy Perkins' has become notoriously prone to mildew, and in recent years has suffered a decline in popularity as a result.

This disease often overwinters in leaf buds near the top of the growth, and also on ramblers generally, especially if they are somewhat neglected. Rosarians usually shorten back their plants around November to prevent wind-rock, so it is a good idea to remove the mildew-infected tips at the same time. Be sure to burn these tips as soon as possible: it may save you much trouble in the following season. Probably the most effective fungicide is the partially systemic benomyl.

ROSE RUST seems to flourish in the same conditions as black spot, so it is most frequently seen in the same areas. Bad attacks, however, affect the plants much more seriously. Varieties bred from 'Fashion' and 'Spartan' (both of which were susceptible but are now seldom planted) seem inclined to infection, and indeed the attractive 'City of Leeds' has become suspect in some areas. The disease is most easily seen in summer, when the bright-orange spores appear as pustules on the undersides of the leaves. These ripen and become black, the leaves crumple and fall, and the plant is seriously weakened. The spraying programme advocated for black spot should give some control. Some rosarians have succeeded in eradicating this disease by using a preparation called 'Plantvax'.

STEM CANKER This disease generally spreads owing to the careless handling of tools, and in severe cases it can cause

Corky calluses due to stem canker

the death of stems of old rose bushes. A corky callus surrounds the stem, preventing the upward flow of the sap. As there is no cure, these cankered stems must be cut off cleanly below the lowest of the cankers, and the diseased material burned. In order to prevent canker, all pruning cuts should be made with a well-sharpened tool capable of making a clean cut. Cultivators, hoes, and mowers should be handled with care to avoid damaging rose bushes.

VIRUS DISEASES have become so common in some plants that they have become a subject of detailed study by horticulturists. Fortunately, they have not yet become so serious a problem on roses in Britain as they have in the United States and Australia. Symptoms of virus are seen in mature leaves, and certain varieties seem more likely to be affected than others; 'Masquerade' and 'Queen Elizabeth' seem to be particularly susceptible.

In vein-banding rose mosaic the pale yellow veins show up in strong contrast to the green leaf. Line-pattern mosaic shows up as pale, wavy lines, sometimes forming an oak-leaf pattern. Some floribundas also show a 'ringspot' infection. As I have mentioned elsewhere, the strawberry ringspot virus is prone to attack *R. rugosa*. There is no means of curing this disease, and where the ringspots appear the stems must be cut off and burned without delay.

Powdery mildew on rose shoots.

The orange spores of rose rust.

15 Exhibitions and Displays

Most gardeners take pride in their work and find it a rewarding experience to visit local, regional, and national shows. For the rose grower there is a special pleasure in visiting the shows mounted by the Royal National Rose Society. For the enthusiastic amateur, there almost inevitably comes a time when he wishes not merely to visit such shows but to take part as an exhibitor. How should he set about it?

Much depends on circumstances, but it is usually best to begin at a fairly modest local level. If you are lucky enough to have an exhibitor friend, you will quickly learn that it is almost as important to keep detailed seasonal records as it is to have green fingers. Good record-keeping is especially important in pruning because exhibition varieties differ considerably in the time they require to produce their blooms at the height of perfection. For instance, the full-petalled roses usually favoured by exhibitors may take as much as 15 or 16 weeks to reach their peak; whereas varieties of moderate petalage will open both earlier and more quickly. (Incidentally, it is true in rose exhibiting, as in other activities, that 'a good big 'un will beat a good little 'un'. This is not because the judges are biased: they are correctly giving recognition to the greater cultural skill which is required to combine size of blooms with quality, perfection of form, and brightness of colour.)

Your records, then, should include reliable information about the exact times that the varieties reach perfection. Such timing, of course, depends partly on where you live and whether the plants are growing in relatively sheltered or exposed areas of your garden. You will almost certainly find that local exhibitors will be pleased to give you basic data and hints on conditions in your area.

Novice exhibitors are usually able to enter their roses in special classes which enable them to gain some experience

before coming up against the skills of the regular exhibitors. At the national rose shows classes are provided for those who grow 1,000 roses, 500, 250, or even less, and there are also classes for an unlimited number of exhibits for those with large gardens. These restrictions are designed to ensure equality of opportunity for growers operating on a large and small scale.

Preparation

When active growth begins frequent, almost daily, attention to your plants becomes vital. Two and sometimes three growths may develop from one eye, and only the most promising should be retained (usually the middle one if three are involved). You should remove the unwanted growths with great care when they are large enough to handle without causing any damage. Some varieties are apt to produce 'blind' growths which will not produce a bloom. Keep a sharp look out for these; if they appear, they should be removed.

Strong growths with promising terminal buds must be staked in those gardens where wind can cause damage (these stakes can be used later if the variety requires protection from rain or sun). Each stem should be limited to one bud, which will develop as the shoot grows. Smaller side buds often appear just below it, and they must be removed as soon as possible without damaging the main or terminal bud. An exception to this practice occurs in the case of a variety that tends to produce 'split' blooms – that is, blooms in which there is a defect in the symmetry of the arrangement of the petals around a well-formed centre, making a break in the circular outline of the

Above left 'Alec's Red' blooms prolifically in summer and autumn and is a popular hybrid tea for exhibition. **Right** Amateur-class winner at an RNRS Summer Show.

Prize-winning 'Embassy' hybrid teas in a typical specimen box at a recent RNRS Summer Show. Boxes of this type are not often seen nowadays at major shows, where more-natural-looking bowls and vases are usually provided by the organizer.

flower. Exhibitors overcome this by removing the terminal bud and taking a side bud which has been spared for this purpose. This results in a smaller but more perfectly shaped flower, usually some days later – which may be an advantage or a disaster, depending on the date of the show.

Cultivation must not be neglected, and should be a matter of routine: a heavy feed just before the show is not likely to produce top-class blooms. Many exhibitors prefer to use liquid fertilizers, which can be more quickly absorbed by the plants; this is often supplemented by foliar feeds. Reliable proprietary brands of fertilizer specially compounded for roses are available. Avoid heavy doses of nitrogen: although it encourages the growth of foliage, on roses its effect flatters to deceive. Potash-rich mixtures are much better, improving the substance of their blooms and enriching the colour of the petals.

Staging

The schedule of the show should always be studied carefully before attempting to stage an exhibit. A visit to the show the previous year will have given you a valuable opportunity to study the class or classes in which you can compete: you will have been able to assess the standard you will need to attain or surpass, and to note the varieties favoured by competitors. You should also have made a point of observing the methods of experienced exhibitors.

Most exhibitors find that some of their blooms require protection from rain or sun, or perhaps both, and special protectors are obtainable for this purpose. They are attached to a stake with a clip which allows adjustment according to the height of the rose stem, and they should be placed in position by the time the blooms are beginning to release their petals. You must take care to ensure that rain cannot drip onto the flower and that wind cannot damage the petals.

Experienced exhibitors tie their buds three days before the show in order to lengthen the petals and so provide a larger and more shapely bloom. This is a useful 'trick of the trade', but you should give yourself plenty of practice before using the method on your exhibits, otherwise you may damage them. Use a piece of thick, soft wool about 230 mm (9 in) long. Pass it around the bloom about two thirds of the way down from the point, and secure it with a double twist. The petals must be quite dry before tying. Blooms already opening should not be tied: they will be past their best before judging time. The ties should be loosened each day to allow for natural growth, otherwise the petals will be marked. Frequent inspection is necessary at this stage, as some blooms may open up too quickly, while others will be backward.

The time for cutting depends largely on how long it will take you to get to the show. If it is a local one and the weather is good, you can get up early the same morning and cut your blooms, placing them immediately in a container of water in a dark, cool place. The stems will absorb water, and this

'Red Lion' hybrid tea in standard show vase.

ing, preferably when the sun is low. Place them in water straight away – preferably in a container in which they can remain until they are placed on the show bench. When cutting, it is a good idea to remove the lower leaves and thorns. Some exhibition varieties suffer from a weak neck and must be supported by wiring to keep the bloom upright. This is another technique the beginner should practise beforehand. Two methods are in general use. One is to push stiff florist's wire into the seed pod and secure it to the stem with wire of a fine gauge. The other method is to use fine-gauge wire to form a small ring around the stem, and then to push it up under the sepals so that it encircles the seed pod; the end of the wire is then run down the stem and twisted around it a couple of times.

Rose blooms (as opposed to the stems) should not be packed wet if you have a long journey to a show. Exhibitors generally develop their own methods, wrapping them in various kinds of soft paper, and designing special boxes to fit into cars or cases. Evolving your own, unique methods is just another part of the fascination of exhibiting. But there is one golden rule when preparing blooms for a long journey: pack them tightly, for if they are allowed any elbow room in the cases they are almost certain to arrive damaged.

Standard items of exhibitor's equipment include a sharp knife, a pen, cards for labelling exhibits, a pair of secateurs, a notebook, your schedule, and reeds or rushes to hold the exhibits in position in their vases. A fine camel-hair brush is also useful for cleaning up and dressing specimen blooms; if moistened it is also the best method of removing any greenfly.

Varieties for exhibition

Hybrid Teas

The qualities looked for are blooms that are three quarters open, with an upright, well-formed centre surrounded by a perfectly symmetrical circle of petals of fine colour. The following are varieties capable of producing blooms of this type; those marked thus ★ are varieties that RNRS records show are exhibitors' favourites.

will keep them fresh for staging. Nowadays most blooms are exhibited in vases or bowls, so stems must be cut long enough for good presentation. At least one basal eye should be left on the plant to provide a new growth for replacement. Specimen blooms are still shown in boxes, and there are usually special classes for this method, although it is now on the decline. For these classes 150 mm (6 in) of stem will be adequate. The boxes measure 450 by 300 mm (18 by 12 in) for six blooms, and 450 by 600 mm (18 by 24 in) for twelve, and have detachable lids. The blooms are inserted in removable holders which fit into water-retaining tubes. Keen exhibitors usually carry a spare box of blooms, so that any which have opened too quickly can be replaced. The decline in the use of specimen boxes is due largely to the increasing popularity of presenting roses more naturally in bowls and vases. These are usually provided at the major shows, whereas exhibition boxes are the property of the exhibitor.

If the journey to the show is going to take you several hours, the blooms will have to be cut the previous even-

★ 'Admiral Rodney'
★ 'Alec's Red'
  'Alpine Sunset'
★ 'Big Chief'
★ 'Bobby Charlton'
  'Bonsoir'
  'Champion'
  'Charlie's Aunt'
★ 'Chicago Peace'
★ 'City of Bath'
★ 'City of Gloucester'
  'Coalite Flame'
★ 'Embassy'
  'Ena Harkness'
★ 'Ernest H. Morse'

★ 'Fragrant Cloud'
★ 'Fred Gibson'
★ 'Gavotte'
★ 'Grandpa Dickson'
  'Honey Favourite'
★ 'Isabel de Ortiz'
  'Jimmy Greaves'
  'John Waterer'
  'Josephine Bruce'
  'McGredy's Yellow'
★ 'Memoriam'
  'My Choice'
  'Northern Lights'
★ 'Peace'
★ 'Perfecta'

★ 'Pink Favourite'
  'Princess'
★ 'Red Devil'
★ 'Red Lion'
  'Rose Gaujard'
★ 'Royal Highness'
  'Silver Lining'
  'Stella'
★ 'Wendy Cussons'

Floribundas

Floribunda roses for exhibition should have young, fresh flowers that are brilliantly coloured and have healthy foliage. As many flowers as possible should be open on each truss, and any aged blooms should be carefully removed, together with their footstalks, using a pair of nail or grape scissors. Some exhibitors believe that the most effective way of achieving large trusses with evenly spaced blooms that open simultaneously is by removing the large central buds and any markedly small buds at an early stage of their development.

The following are some of the varieties that have predominated at major shows in the last year or so. Three floribundas that are usually classified as shrubs but are eligible for exhibition in this class are marked thus ★.

  'Anna Wheatcroft'
  'Anne Cocker'
  'Arthur Bell'
  'Chanelle'
  'City of Leeds'
  'Dearest'
★ 'Dorothy Wheatcroft'
  'Elizabeth of Glamis'
  'Escapade'
  'Evelyn Fison'
★ 'Fred Loads'
  'Iceberg'
★ 'Lavender Lassie'
  'Lili Marlene'
  'Megiddo'
  'Molly McGredy'
  'Ohlala'
  'Orangeade'
  'Pink Elizabeth Arden'
  'Pink Parfait'
  'Queen Elizabeth'
  'Redgold'
  'Scented Air'
  'Sea Pearl'
  'Southampton'

A class-winning bowl of mixed floribundas at an RNRS Summer Show.

Permanent displays

Roses are best seen in permanent gardens, which give a much better idea of their potential for general display than you can get at nurseries, where the plants are all maidens. (Some nurseries do, of course, have their own display gardens, which offer equally good opportunities for you to assess the qualities of mature plants.) The following are a few of the best places to see permanent displays in the United Kingdom.

Queen Mary's Garden, at Regent's Park in London, is considered to be one of the outstanding gardens for rose display in this country. (Modesty forbids me to say anything more, as it was under my care for about 15 years.) It contains about 40,000 plants, some in large formal beds, many in fixed borders. A large collection of climbers and ramblers forms a background to the main formal garden, and many more scramble into trees.

The Royal Botanic Gardens at Kew have an interesting collection of roses in beds of various sizes, and includes examples of pegging down of older varieties in beds. A large pergola displays a selection of climbers.

The Royal National Rose Society's Garden in Chiswell Green Lane, on the outskirts of St Albans, provides an opportunity for members of the society and visitors to see the widest range of roses in the British Isles from June to September. The roses range from species and their hybrids, through the old garden roses, modern shrubs, and climbers, to modern hybrid teas, floribundas, and miniatures. A large pergola provides a display of climbers old and new. In the trial grounds roses from all over the world – no doubt including many future favourites – can be seen. Award-winning roses from these trials are planted at selected gardens in various parts of the country to assess their performance under different climatic conditions. These gardens – all of them well worth a visit in any case – are at: Roath Park, Cardiff; Saughton Park, Edinburgh; Pollock Park, Glasgow; Harlow Car Gardens, near Harrogate, North Yorkshire; Heigham Park, Norwich; The Arboretum, Nottingham; Borough Park, Redcar, Cleveland; Rotten Row, Victoria Park, Southport, Lancashire; Vivary Park, Taunton, Somerset. The City of Belfast Rose Trials Gardens at the Sir Thomas and Lady Dinon Park, just outside the city, has a splendid collection of more than 20,000 plants of different types, including shrub roses.

In recent years the Royal Horticultural Society has created a display of modern roses at its garden at Wisley, in Surrey. Older roses are also grown in other parts of the garden.

Many public parks and gardens all over Britain provide evidence of our enduring love of roses. They are far too numerous to identify here by name or place, but I should perhaps mention the city of Aberdeen's reputation for outstanding displays of roses, and also the National Trust, many of whose gardens have splendid collections of the older roses.

The RNRS gardens at St Albans are outstanding among hundreds of rose gardens all over Britain that can be visited by the enthusiast.

16 Roses as Cut Flowers

ROSES, in spite of a comparatively short life when cut, are always much in demand for decoration at public and private functions. They are grown for this purpose by highly specialized growers, under glass – in the border soil, not in pots – and the varieties are specially selected for their ability to crop at different seasons. Length of stem, size of flower, lasting quality, and colour are the properties looked for (scent does not seem to be so important). 'Baccara' has long been noted for its value in this field, being deep geranium-red in colour; but it is of little value for outside growing. More recently 'Sweet Promise' ('Sonia') has also become popular.

A floribunda rose named 'Garnette' has given rise to a distinct category of roses whose small, full flowers last especially well when cut. The plants are dwarf in habit, about 380 mm (15 in) high, and may be grown outdoors, but they are primarily 'forcing' roses which produce the best results when grown under glass. The original 'Garnette' (so named, presumably, because of its garnet-red flowers) has also produced some sports, of which the following are a selection.
'Garnette Apricot' (yellow with pink shading)
'Garnette Carol' (clear pink)
'Garnette Pink Chiffon' (clear pale pink)
'Garnette Rose' (deep carmine-pink)
'Garnette Yellow' (pale yellow)

Most readers of this book are more likely to try to produce flowers for cutting from plants grown also for their decorative value in the garden, or perhaps in an area in the vegetable garden specially set aside for the purpose. In general, medium-sized blooms of good shape and petals of good substance are best. Stems should be of good length, slender but strong enough to carry the flower erect, fairly free of thorns, and possessing attractive foliage.

The colour should be clear, free from bleaching or burning by the sun, as resistant as possible to weather damage, and should not fade to an objectionable shade. Scent is more important to some growers than to others, but it certainly adds to the pleasure cut roses can give. Many keen rose lovers find a special delight in one perfect rose placed in a specimen vase; here, I am sure, the effect is enhanced by fragrance.

Care of cut roses

The ideal time for cutting roses is late evening, just before dew begins to form, or early in the morning. When cut the roses should be placed in a container with enough water to enable the foliage and stem to be immersed almost up to the flowerhead. Proprietary mixtures are available containing dextrose, alum, and other ingredients which may help to prolong the life of the flower. If you use one of these mixtures the flowers must be put in it from the start, and not switched to plain water or vice-versa. It is a good idea to have a second container full of the mixture, to which the roses can be transferred one at a time after you have removed all leaves and thorns likely to be immersed when the flowers are placed in a bowl or vase. Leave the container in a cool place for some hours, preferably in the dark, before setting up your arrangement.

Sometimes roses wilt, especially if they are packed dry for several hours in hot weather. They can be revived by cutting a small piece of the stem away, placing the remaining stem in about 25 mm (1 in) of boiling or very hot water for 30 seconds, and then filling up the container with cold water as near as possible to the neck of the

Above left 'Anne Cocker' is one of the longer-lasting floribundas when used as a cut flower. **Right** Pleasantly scented, 'Vera Dalton' blooms are well set off by their glossy, dark-green leaves.

A selection of garnette roses, whose beauty and long-lasting quality have made them among the most popular roses used as cut flowers.

bloom. Within an hour or so the flower should have recovered.

Most people have their own ideas about the kind of receptacle they like to use. Perhaps the most attractive are of copper, silver, wood, or cut glass. As long as they are of good shape and deep enough to hold plenty of water, they will be satisfactory. Personally, I prefer simple designs, so that nothing detracts from the roses themselves.

The introduction of Oasis, a rigid but spongy green material which absorbs a lot of water and is available in block form, has helped greatly in the arrangement of roses and other cut flowers. When thoroughly soaked in water the blocks can usually be fitted into a container, but as they are light they must be fixed or tied to prevent them falling over. Stems can then be placed exactly where required and usually remain fresh for two days.

Selection

Most rosarians have particular favourites, so it is with some diffidence that I recommend the following for cutting:

Hybrid Teas
'Alexander'
'Blessings'
'Blue Moon'
'Elizabeth Harkness' (especially in autumn or as a specimen)
'Fragrant Cloud' (best colour in autumn)
'Korp' (a small, neat flower of pure vermilion)
'Mme Butterfly' (an old-timer but still good)
'Ophelia' (for many years a great favourite)
'Papa Meilland' (good as a single specimen)
'Pascali'
'Super Star' (good but prone to mildew)
'Sutter's Gold'
'Wendy Cussons' (especially good under artificial light)
'Whisky Mac'

Floribundas
'Anne Cocker' (lasts well)
'Apricot Nectar'
'Arthur Bell'
'Copper Pot'
'Dearest'
'Elizabeth of Glamis'
'Esther Ofarim' (particularly good for forcing under glass)
'Glenfiddich' (for those who live in cooler areas)
'Iceberg'
'Iced Ginger'
'Margaret Merril' (especially for fragrance)
'Moon Maiden'
'Paddy McGredy'
'Pink Parfait'
'Queen Elizabeth' (ideal for large arrangements)
'Sea Pearl'
'Sunsilk'
'Vera Dalton'

Unusual colours

In recent years some roses, mainly floribundas, have been raised not because of their value for garden decoration but because of their unusual colours, which have become of great interest to flower arrangers. The following are a selection:

'Amberlight' (large, semi-double flowers, clear golden brown turning to buff, and sweetly scented)

'Artistic' (wiry stems, golden brown flowers fading to soft salmon)

'Brownie' (golden yellow, pink, and bronze)

'Café' (shades of coffee and cream)

'Grey Dawn' (double, soft-grey flowers)

'Jocelyn' (very double, flat flowers of mahogany, passing to purplish brown)

'Lilac Charm' (lilac with golden anthers; keep away from bright sunlight)

'Maud Cole' (beautiful foliage; wine-red and deep-violet petals)

'Ripples' (lilac, with unusual waved petals)

'Silver Charm' (resembles 'Lilac Charm', but less liable to fade)

'Tom Brown' (two-toned brown)

'Vesper' (soft orange-brown; inclined to fade in hot weather)

Attractive foliage

In mixed arrangements of roses it can be very effective to use foliage from some rose species which have particularly attractive leaves. Classes at specialist rose shows are often provided for such exhibits, of which the most popular is *Rosa rubrifolia*, an easily grown shrub which is also of great garden value. Its leaves are unique in their glaucous, copper-mauve colouring. The best foliage for decoration is invariably on young growths produced in the previous year. Old wood should be pruned away to encourage such growths. Popular also, but in a different way, is *R. sericea pteracantha*, a species valued for its ferny leaves and for its large, red, translucent thorns, which are produced on the current year's growth. Again, therefore, pruning away of old wood is necessary to produce the required growths. If soft, its stem should be soaked thoroughly beforehand which will ensure it remains upright.

Daintiest of all roses, surely, is *R. farreri persetosa*, the 'three-penny-bit rose', whose ferny grace will embellish any arrangement and is equally attractive in the garden. It is even more alluring when its tiny salmon-pink flowers appear in conjunction with coral-pink buds.

Another attractive species is *R. fedtschenkoana*, which produces young grey shoots with pink, bristly thorns and pale grey-green leaves, although on a shrub too large for small gardens. *R. willmottiae* produces young growths with tinted thorns that create a pinkish effect, contrasting with its tiny greyish leaves. *R. × pteragonis* 'Cantabrigiensis' grows into a large, free-flowering shrub suitable only for a largish garden. Where room can be found, however, its fine fern-like foliage can be used effectively with cut roses. Its creamy yellow blooms appear in late May.

The fruits of many roses are highly decorative in themselves and add greatly to autumn arrangements.

A bowl of miniature roses: 'Lavender Lace', 'Judy Fischer' (deep pink), 'Easter Morning' (ivory), 'Fire Princess' (brilliant red), 'Yellow Doll', 'Toy Clown' (pinkish-red and white), and 'Little Flirt' (orange-red and gold).

17 The Rose-Grower's Year

THIS monthly calendar of tasks should be used only as a reminder and for general guidance. Rigid timetables cannot be set out because the climate varies considerably in different parts of the country and from one year to the next, so rosarians should adapt suggestions to suit their own local conditions.

January

The hours of daylight are short and inclement weather is likely to disorganize your plans, but planting of roses can continue when soil and weather conditions permit. Treading of heavy soil should be avoided if it is very wet. Shrub roses may be pruned if hard frosts are not prevalent. Roses grown under glass should be given enough heat to keep out frost, but allowed some ventilation by day.

February

Floribunda roses may now be pruned, particularly in southern and sheltered gardens. In areas where black spot or mildew cause problems, spray roses with a copper fungicide such as Bordeaux Mixture. Stocks budded last year can now be headed back. Canes should be inserted to indicate their position; these will also provide support for young growth in due course. Roses under glass will benefit from a spray of clear water early in the day when the weather is fair.

March

Always a busy month if the weather is good. In all but northern and exposed gardens, pruning should be completed by the end of the month; burn all pruned material. Late planting should also be finished. Stocks should be planted now if budding is planned. All beds where roses are grown on their own should be thoroughly weeded; if you have no time for weeding, water the beds with a weedkiller based on simazine. Roses under glass should be sprayed for protection against greenfly. Encourage their growth by applying a liquid fertilizer once a week and raising the greenhouse temperature.

April

All pruning should have been completed. Apply rose fertilizer to your outdoor plants. Check the standards to see that their ties and supports are secure. Exhibitors should check on pruning cuts and rub out surplus growths; if only the lower eyes have started to develop, remove the wood above them. Fumigate the greenhouse as an additional protection against greenfly. Damp down the pathways and the benching between pots on hot days. Provide shade if necessary for any early blooms.

May

Those who grow shrub roses can begin to enjoy them this month. Greenfly generally makes its first attack early in the month and should be controlled by spraying. A mixture of systemic insecticide and systemic fungicide should take care of other pests and diseases. If you use foliar feeds, you can begin to apply them now, especially to backward plants. Tie back growths from last year's budding to supporting canes. Pot plants which are finishing flowering can be stood outside, especially if space is short in the greenhouse. Now is the time to mulch rose beds with garden compost or farmyard manure while the soil is still moist.

June

In southern gardens roses should be coming into flower. If large blooms are required, particularly for exhibition, disbudding of small or surplus buds will be necessary. Exhibitors must now study their schedules, get their equipment ready, and notify the show committees if they intend to participate. In some areas watering, particularly of late-planted roses, may now be necessary. All pot roses can now be stood outside.

Like other shrub roses 'Penelope' should be pruned in January This fine hybrid musk was raised by Rev G H Pemberton in 1924.

July

In general, throughout the country, this is the best month to enjoy roses. If you are interested in new roses, visit the trial grounds of the Royal National Rose Society at St Albans or the other gardens mentioned in Chapter 15. Rose shows should also be visited, as well as specialist rose nurserymen, particularly those in your own area. Dead-heading should begin, cutting back to the first or second eye below. Another application of rose fertilizer will be beneficial. Spray again if necessary with insecticide and fungicide. Bud your stocks if they are ready.

August

Another good month for seeing roses everywhere, and a great time for shows, local and national. The trial gardens will have especially fine displays of autumn floribundas. New varieties can be seen at rose nurseries, where they can be selected and ordered.

September

The month of the autumn shows, that of the RNRS in particular. Climber or rambler roses that have finished flowering should now be pruned, and young growths tied in after the removal of flowering growths. Rose cuttings can be taken and inserted towards the end of the month. In some areas, black spot will require further fungicidal treatment.

Above July and August are the best months to visit rose trial grounds, such as this nurseryman's, to make a note of possible future favourites.

October

This month is really the beginning of the rose-grower's year. New beds should be prepared, and (if it has not already been done) new roses should be ordered. Nurserymen usually start lifting this month, so if you ordered early you may be able to plant before the month is out. Roses in pots should be checked over and repotted if necessary. New varieties can be potted up either from the garden or from a nursery.

The attractive autumn hips of *Rosa holodonta*.

November

This is generally the time to plant out new roses unless early rains make the ground too sticky. Long growths on established roses should be shortened during this month to prevent wind rock. Pot roses can be brought under glass. Many rosarians, especially those in the milder areas of the country, favour pruning now in order to get earlier displays next year. Beginners, however, should be influenced by local conditions and should take advice before making such a decision.

December

Preparation and planting can be continued this month, heeling in any roses where the soil is very wet. In frosty weather put out straw or bracken to protect very exposed plants. Climbers not dealt with earlier can be pruned now. Roses in pots should be pruned at the end of the month. Fallen rose leaves, particularly those attacked by black spot, should be raked up and burned. If the ground is not too wet it should be prepared now for your spring planting.

Index

Acknowledgments

The publishers thank the following organisations and individuals for their kind permission to reproduce the photographs in this book:

A–Z Botanical Collection Limited 28 below, 45, 48, 50 above right, 51, 61 below; Bernard Alfieri 17, 18; Biofotos (H.M. le Rougetel) 44, 54; Pat Brindley 19, 46, 53 below right, 59, 60, 61 above right, 80 below right, 90, 91; Nigel Browne 71; Bruce Coleman Limited 5, 11, 79, 88, 94; Eric Crichton 13, 30, 87; Graham Dickinson 26 below; Valerie Finnis 70; C. Gregory & Sons Limited 7; George Hyde 78, 81 below left; Jarrold & Sons Limited 31; Leslie Johns & Associates 93; S. Millar Gault 50 below right; Malcolm Robertson 21; Royal Horticultural Society's Garden, Wisley 80 centre, 81 below centre and above right; Royal National Rose Society 29 below, 43, 64, 74, 83, 84, 85, 86, 95; Harry Smith Horticultural Photographic Collection 2, 9, 10, 12 above and below left, 28 above left, 33 below, 37, 38 above left, 41, 47, 52, 55, 58, 62, 63, 67, 69, 77 above left, 82, 89; Spectrum Colour Library 14; Pamla Toler 1, 15, 24, 25, 26 above, 27, 29 above right, 32, 33 above, 34, 35, 36, 38 below left, 39, 40, 49, 53 above right, 57, 65 above and below right, 75, 77 below left; Wheatcroft Roses Limited 23.